101 Advanced Spreadsheet Exercises

Using Lotus 1-2-3, VP-Planner, and Twin

Lloyd D. Brooks

Professor and Chairman, Department of Management
  Information Systems and Decision Sciences
Fogelman College of Business and Economics
Memphis State University
Memphis, Tennessee

Gregg Division
McGRAW-HILL PUBLISHING COMPANY

New York Atlanta Dallas St. Louis San Francisco Auckland
Bogotá Caracas Hamburg Lisbon London
Madrid Mexico Milan Montreal New Delhi Paris
San Juan São Paulo Singapore Sydney Tokyo Toronto

Sponsoring Editor: **Arthur Pomponio**
Editing Supervisor: **Mitsy Kovacs**
Design and Art Supervisor: **Meri Shardin**
Production Supervisor: **Kathleen Donnelly**

Text Designer: **Phyllis Lerner and Renée Kilbride Edelman**
Cover Designer: **Peter Weber**

ACKNOWLEDGMENTS
The author is grateful to the following reviewers who supplied valuable expertise during the development of this book: Mike Michaelson, Associate Professor of Computer Information Systems, Palomar College (University of California at San Diego) and Wally M. Guyot, Chairman, Department of Business Education and Office Administration, Fort Hays State University.

Lotus 1-2-3 is a registered trademark of Lotus Development Corporation. VP Planner is a registered trademark of Paperback Software International. Twin is a registered trademark of Mosaic Software, Inc.

101 Advanced Spreadsheet Exercises

1 2 3 4 5 6 7 8 9 0   SEMSEM   8 9 6 5 4 3 2 1 0 9

ISBN 0-07-008186-7

Contents

FILE MAINTENANCE AND MISCELLANEOUS

DECISION MAKING

MACRO DEVELOPMENT

DATABASE MANAGEMENT

Introduction

101 Advanced Spreadsheet Exercises provides a series of short exercises covering electronic spreadsheet applications. It can be used with any microcomputer and any integrated spreadsheet package. However, the tutorial and optional data disk are designed for the IBM (or compatible) microcomputer and the Lotus 1-2-3 software package (or clones such as VP-Planner and Twin). Although a majority of the exercises are concerned with related spreadsheet applications, exercises relating to database and graphics applications are also included.

The exercises are grouped into nine areas: Overview of Basics; Appearance of Reports; Functions: Date, Mathematical, Financial, and Statistical; File Maintenance and Miscellaneous; Decision Making; Macro Development; Database Management; Graphing; and Extended Spreadsheet Templates. Within each area, the exercises are arranged by function from the simpler to the more complex. All sections, with the exception of Extended Spreadsheet Templates, end with an integrated reinforcement exercise to support previously learned skills. You will learn spreadsheet applications and functions from short exercises containing typical business examples.

An Overview of Basics section is provided for people with limited instruction in spreadsheet applications, or for people who have had instruction but need a review. However, people with introductory spreadsheet skills will be able to complete the program more easily and benefit from the advanced concepts and applications included in the program.

Before you begin, a review of the equipment and available software may be necessary. Although the tutorial contains the necessary commands and instructions for completing the exercises, your software manual and directions from your instructor may be helpful when questions arise.

GENERAL INSTRUCTIONS

Terminology Many different electronic spreadsheet software packages are currently available. Although they vary in capacity, the general layout, terminology, and design are similar. With only a few exceptions, the terminology used in this text will match that of your software, whatever it may be. Spreadsheet programs are variously referred to as "spreadsheets," "electronic spreadsheets," or "worksheets." This text uses the term "worksheet" to refer to a template. If a term is unfamiliar

to you, refer to the Glossary at the front of the book, check your software manual, or ask your instructor.

Default Most spreadsheets have preset responses, or defaults, which vary from one program to another. For example, many spreadsheets have either 0 or 2 as the decimal default for the number of places to the right of the decimal point. Another typical default is for files to automatically be saved to a particular disk drive, such as Drive A. Spreadsheet defaults can be changed. The required number of decimal places, column widths, and other formatting requirements will be indicated in the exercise instructions or by a review of the spreadsheet template shown in the exercise.

Exercise Sheets Each exercise is presented on an exercise sheet. After completing the exercise, submit the sheet with the required printed material to your instructor for grading or review. (Your instructor may give you special instructions about submitting your work.)

When you are instructed in an exercise to write formulas in the blanks, do so before entering the formulas in the spreadsheet. Enter data in the rows and columns indicated in the exercise. The format, layout, and design of printed copies should be similar to those of the examples shown on the exercise sheets unless you are otherwise instructed.

Functions   This text includes typical functions used in a variety of spreadsheet packages. If you need more information about a particular function, consult the user's manual for your software or ask your instructor for assistance.

Clearing the Screen   After completing an exercise, you should clear the information from the monitor and from memory prior to completing the next exercise. When you are instructed to save a spreadsheet, save it prior to clearing the screen.

Spacing   Vary column widths, when needed, to make the appearance as attractive and functional as possible.

Tutorial   A tutorial is included in this workbook to provide instructions, menu commands, and helpful hints needed to complete the exercises. Detailed instructions will be given when a new function is introduced. Functions will often be repeated, with little or no additional explanation, in later exercises for reinforcement. It is important that you notice changes in your menus and screen as you execute commands in order to learn the operations being performed. Tutorial instructions relate to Lotus 1-2-3 but can be applied to clones such as VP-Planner and Twin. The tutorial can serve as a learning aid and reference.

Data Disk   Many of the templates have been partially entered and stored on the "optional" data disk. Files have been stored in a directory named A101. When you are given the option of retrieving a file for an exercise, you can easily retrieve the template from the directory. After a few exercises, you will find the directory to be easy to use. The files can be stored on a floppy disk, a hard drive, or a network. More specific instructions for using the directory are given in the tutorial. Files that you create can be stored in the directory, individually on the disk, or in a separate directory that you create. Ask your instructor about the preferred procedures. If your instructor has chosen not to use the optional data disk in your class, you should enter each template in its entirety as part of the exercise.

Occasionally, you will be requested to save a file for use in a later exercise. Be sure to save these completed exercises, as directed. For other exercises, ask your instructor about the policy for saving these exercises on disk or hard drive.

Glossary

absolute reference A method of replication which prevents cell contents contained in formulas from changing when the formulas are copied.

alphanumeric entry An entry consisting of any combination of letters, numbers, symbols, and/or spaces.

ascending The sequence of sorting which moves from low to high.

ASCII file A text file which can be created from a spreadsheet and then used with other software applications or can be created using other software and then imported into a spreadsheet.

automatic execution macro A special macro (0) which is invoked automatically when a spreadsheet is loaded.

axis titles Graph titles which can appear below the horizontal axis or to the left of the vertical axis.

bar graph A type of graph which uses the lengths of bars to represent numeric value relationships.

borders Specific rows and/or columns which print on each page of a report.

cell The space formed by the intersection of a column and a row and thus a place where data can be entered on a spreadsheet.

cell address The location of a cell in the spreadsheet.

cell pointer The cursor which indicates screen position on a spreadsheet.

character Any letter, number, or symbol (including space) which can be displayed on the screen.

column width The number of positions (spaces) allocated to a column for display on the screen and subsequent printing. Column width is often preset to 9 spaces.

copy See *replicate*.

criteria Standards used to specify which records are to be affected by a process, such as extracting or deleting.

data table A table containing sequences of numbers.

database A group of related records.

decimal place The position to the right of a decimal point.

default A predetermined setting, such as a default column width of 9 positions.

descending The sequence of sorting which moves from high to low.

directory A structured file management scheme in which files can be organized into groups called directories.

display The screen or monitor.

extracting Selecting specified database records and copying them into an extraction range for viewing and/or printing.

file A block of information which can be stored on a disk, retrieved to be used again, or deleted. Files must be assigned names when they are stored.

finding Selecting specified database records for viewing on the screen.

footer A line of information that prints at the bottom of each page.

format The setup of data display. In the Currency Format, for example, values usually appear with dollar signs, commas, and 2 decimal places.

function A simplified way of executing long or complicated formulas or processes—for example, using the @SUM function to add an entire range of cells instead of entering each cell address.

global That which affects the entire spreadsheet, such as global column width.

graph A pictorial illustration of data relationships, such as a line graph.

header A line of information that prints at the top of each page.

information system A system that takes and processes data, and provides information as output.

integer A whole-number positive or negative value. Integers appear without decimal points.

intelligent macro A macro which produces varying results depending on specified conditions being met.

interactive pause macro A macro which pauses and allows the user to input cell entries or responses as the macro is being executed.

labels See *text entry*.

label-prefix A symbol appearing in front of a cell entry to indicate the alignment of the cell contents.

left-alignment The position of alphanumeric text in which cell entries are vertically lined up along the left side of the cell.

legend A variety of pattern symbols used in a bar graph to distinguish the multiple bars.

line graph A type of graph using lines to illustrate data relationships.

logical connective AND and OR used in formulas to establish conditions to be met by the results of the calculation. If AND is used, both conditions must be true. If OR is used, one or the other condition must be true.

logical operators The symbols (=, <, >, <=, >=, <>) used in formulas to establish relationships between values.

lookup The process used with tables of data to search for corresponding values in specified rows or columns of the table.

macro A method of storing a sequence of keystrokes in conjunction with a single key on the keyboard.

master macro A macro which is created, saved, and retrieved to be used in multiple spreadsheets.

menu A list of choices from which the user makes a selection.

monitor A display or screen.

network A system whereby two or more communication devices (such as microcomputers) are connected to one another.

numeric entry See *values*.

overwriting Replacing an original file which has already been given a name with a revised version under the same name.

parenthesis hierarchy A system whereby portions of a formula are contained in parentheses to ensure that these calculations will be performed first.

pie chart A type of graph which displays data relationships as segments of a pie or circle.

prompt An indicator on the screen showing that the computer is waiting to receive a user response.

protection The process of ensuring that cells are not modified inadvertently.

range A group of cells forming a vertical or horizontal rectangular block (a range may even consist of a single cell).

recalculation The automatic recalculation performed when cell entries are changed in a spreadsheet unless manual recalculation is specified.

record A single group of related data items in a database, such as the information about one client or product.

relative reference A method of replication in which a formula changes relative to each column or row. For example, +A1+B1 becomes +A2+B2 when copied from row 1 to row 2.

replacement The alteration of the contents of a cell by entering new information in place of old; also called "strike-over."

replicate A function that copies cell contents from one range of cells to another (also called *copy*).

retrieve A function that loads or recalls a file from disk storage.

right-alignment The position of alphanumeric text or values in which cell entries are vertically lined up along the right side of the cell.

scale   The range of numeric values appearing on the horizontal and/ or vertical axis of a graph.

screen   The display or monitor.

scroll   To roll the spreadsheet on the screen vertically or horizontally.

sequence   The order or arrangement of records in a database.

software   Programs that control the operation of the computer system. The words "software" and "program" are used interchangeably.

sorting   The process of arranging database records in a specified sequence on the basis of designated criteria or keys.

spreadsheet   A set of columns or rows into which data are entered and organized. Calculations and other functions can be performed on the data. Also called "worksheet."

statistical function   A special function used in conjunction with speadsheet values or database records to analyze numbers to establish patterns or for performing calculations on specified records only, such as @DSUM and @STD.

strike-over   See *replacement*.

text entry   A word or number entered as a label.

titles   Main or column headings frozen vertically or horizontally so that they will not scroll off the screen.

values   Numeric entries that can be used in calculations.

window   An area of a spreadsheet that can be displayed on the screen at any given time.

worksheet   See *spreadsheet*.

XY graph   A type of graph or scatterplot which illustrates a trend in data by plotting values for both the vertical and horizontal axes.

Name _____ Date _____ Section _____ Evaluation _____

EXERCISE 1   Entering Text and Values

- Enter the information in columns A to D as shown below. (Note: Right-align the data in column B.)

```
       A        B       C        D        E        F        G        H
 1   Name     ID No.  Age      Salary
 2   ====================================
 3   Cole, B.   218P    32     252.87
 4   Doer, G.   316P    34     345.88
 5   Erwin, E.  452I    21     309.32
 6   Harms, M.  381Y    19     319.43
 7   Hovey, P.  429F    47     420.35
 8   Huang, L.  375N    51     275.02
 9   Mott, D.   619B    62     290.22
10   Shas, W.   483C    24     314.25
11   ====================================
```

- In the spaces below answer the following questions:
  1. What age is Harms, M.? _____
  2. Which employee had the highest salary? _____
  3. How many employees are older than 25? _____
  4. What is the name of the oldest employee? _____
  5. What is the name of the youngest employee? _____

EXERCISE 2 — Using Label Prefixes and Saving a File

- Enter the information in columns A to D as shown below.
- Enter the label prefix needed to center the headings in columns A and C.
- Enter the label prefix needed to right-align the headings in columns B and D.

```
        A         B         C        D        E       F       G       H
1   Employee  Employee    Sales   Years of
2     Name        ID     Amount   Service
3   ========================================
4   Barns, J.    325     674.67        9
5   Brady, T.    278     713.44       13
6   Cofer, P.    215     784.62        2
7   Dell, R.     344     567.33       16
8   Otto, J.     903     643.72        8
9   Park, O.     251     462.88       23
10  Rich, S.     325     519.48       13
11  Ruoff, P.    523     627.42       19
12  Rusk, D.     174     578.32       25
13  Shell, W.    345     698.05       12
14  Theis, M.    214     562.78        5
15  Wills, C.    230     625.78       13
16  ========================================
```

- Save the worksheet with the following file name: <u>EXER2</u>
- In the spaces below answer the following questions:

  1. Which employee had the largest sales amount?

  _____

  2. If employees can retire after 25 years of service, how many employees are eligible for retirement benefits? _____

  3. What label prefix was used for the heading for column D?

  _____

  4. What label prefix was used for the heading for column A?

  _____

  5. How many employees had sales amounts over $600?

  _____

EXERCISE 3

Retrieving and Printing a Worksheet

- Retrieve the worksheet created in Exercise 2. Remember that the file name is EXER2. The worksheet should appear like the one shown below.

	A	B	C	D	E	F	G	H
1	Employee	Employee	Sales	Years of				
2	Name	ID	Amount	Service				
3	===================================							
4	Barns, J.	325	674.67	9				
5	Brady, T.	278	713.44	13				
6	Cofer, P.	215	784.62	2				
7	Dell, R.	344	567.33	16				
8	Otto, J.	903	643.72	8				
9	Park, O.	251	462.88	23				
10	Rich, S.	325	519.48	13				
11	Ruoff, P.	523	627.42	19				
12	Rusk, D.	174	578.32	25				
13	Shell, W.	345	698.05	12				
14	Theis, M.	214	562.78	5				
15	Wills, C.	230	625.78	13				
16	===================================							

- Print one copy of the worksheet.
- Change Mr. Cofer's years of service to 24.
- Change Ms. Dell's Employee ID to 324.
- Save the file with the following file name: EXER3
- Print one copy of the report.

OVERVIEW OF BASICS

Name _____ Date _____ Section _____ Evaluation _____

EXERCISE 4 Using the Help Facility with Lotus 1-2-3

- Access the Help Facility.
- Read the text on the screen.
- Press <PgDn> and read the screen. Answer the following questions:
  1. What key should be pressed to go to the upper left corner of the worksheet? _____
  2. What key should be pressed to move the worksheet to the right one screen? _____
- Press <F1> to display the Help Index.
- Press <F5> then type 11 then press <Return> to view Mathematical Operators. Answer the following questions:
  3. What is the operator for the "Exponentiation" Function?

     _____
  4. What is the operator for the "Greater Than" Function?

     _____
  5. What is the operator for the "Addition" Function?

     _____
- Press <F1> then press <F5> then type 18 then press <Return> to view Financial Functions. Answer the following questions:
  6. What is the format for computing a periodic payment?

     _____
  7. What is the format for computing present value?

     _____
- Press <F1> then press <F5> then type 19 then press <Return> for more Financial Functions. Answer the following question:
  8. What is the format for net present value? _____
- Press <Esc> to exit the Help Facility and return to the worksheet.

EXERCISE 5 Formatting Values

- Enter the information in columns A to E as shown below. (Option: Retrieve file EXER5.)

	A	B	C	D	E	F	G	H
1	1423.82	0.189	284.16	2748.329	1428.829			
2	2341.22	0.231	437.33	4326.78	45.348			
3	7283.33	0.326	546.33	4525.7	15.783			
4	384.21	0.34	738.86	523.53	2643.4			
5	219.32	0.46	854.347	5.679	6734.56			
6	4232.56	0.8	56.88	5.5	3452.45			
7	2340.46	0.428	543.89	3428.41	56.7284			
8	3265.49	0.352	6.8953	5.6274	5.8756			
9	2341.45	0.358	6.4327	6.734	345.72			
10	3.67	0.394	573.85	2.876	381.209			
11	2.43	0.261	385.36	8437.34	2456.871			
12	167.33	0.426	327.823	345.71	3534.787			
13	23.56	0.404	7.5658	5434.85	562.45			
14	23.44	0.782	4.56	923.446	5.6			
15	3.49	0.897	4.82	5.8193	5.34			

- Format column A for fixed format with 1 decimal place.
- Format column B for percent format with 1 decimal place.
- Format column C for currency format with 2 decimal places.
- Format column D for comma format with 2 decimal places.
- Format column E for comma format with 1 decimal place.
- Save the file with the following file name: EXER5
  (Note: You will choose the "Replace" option when saving files which have currently existing file names on the disk.)
- Print one copy of the report.

EXERCISE 6   Entering Formulas

OVERVIEW OF BASICS

- Enter the information in columns A to C as shown below. (Option: Retrieve file <u>EXER6</u>.)

	A	B	C	D	E	F	G	H
1	5.74	12.45	234.43					
2	6.83	32.54	435.67					
3	7.45	28.19	352.45					
4	3.24	36.23	453.46					
5	5.34	28.43	532.23					
6	4.54	38.43	346.18					
7	5.67	29.83	325.65					
8	4.56	74.92	428.54					
9	5.32	54.28	536.75					
10	5.29	32.36	475.55					

- In the spaces below write the formulas needed to perform the following computations in column D.

Computation	Formula
Subtract cell B1 from the sum of cells A1 and C1.	D1 _____
Divide cell B2 by cell A2 and subtract the result from cell C2.	D2 _____
Multiply cell A3 by cell B3.	D3 _____
Divide cell C4 by cell A4.	D4 _____
Divide the sum of cells A5 and C5 by cell B5.	D5 _____
Raise cell A6 to the second power.	D6 _____
Subtract the sum of cell A7 and cell B7 from the sum of cell B7 and cell C7.	D7 _____
Compute the square root of cell C8.	D8 _____
Multiply cell B9 by 23.	D9 _____
Add the square root of cell C10 to the square root of cell B10.	D10 _____

- Enter the formulas in the worksheet.
- Print one copy of the table.

EXERCISE 7

Using Functional Formulas

- Enter the following information in columns A to H as shown below. (Option: Retrieve file EXER7.)

```
          A         B         C         D         E         F         G         H
1    Sales Report
2
3    Name      Mon.      Tue.      Wed.      Thur.     Fri.      Totals    Averages
4    -----------------------------------------------------------------------------
5    Abel      289.34    354.36    234.43    376.46    356.38
6    Collins   345.65    365.45    209.45    256.45    265.45
7    Doak      245.54    387.98    234.45    378.13    401.23
8    Jolly     254.34    245.45    245.45    354.46    245.32
9    Magnini   234.54    342.44    267.23    242.61    265.78
10   Nguyen    264.34    434.56    278.54    367.43    345.61
11   -----------------------------------------------------------------------------
12   Totals
13   Averages
14   High
15   Low
16   -----------------------------------------------------------------------------
```

- In the spaces below write the formulas needed to compute the appropriate amounts (using functional formulas).

  G5 _____   B13 _____

  H5 _____   B14 _____

  B12 _____   B15 _____

- Enter the formulas in the worksheet in the above cell addresses only.
- Save the file with the following file name: EXER7
- Print one copy of the report.

OVERVIEW OF BASICS

EXERCISE 8 Copying Formulas

OVERVIEW OF BASICS

- Enter the following information in columns A to H as shown below. (Option: Retrieve file <u>EXER7</u>.) Note: This file was created and saved as part of the previous exercise.

```
         A          B          C          D          E          F          G          H
 1   Sales Report
 2
 3   Name       Mon.       Tue.       Wed.       Thur.      Fri.       Totals     Averages
 4   ------------------------------------------------------------------------------------
 5   Abel       289.34     354.36     234.43     376.46     356.38     1610.97    322.194
 6   Collins    345.65     365.45     209.45     256.45     265.45
 7   Doak       245.54     387.98     234.45     378.13     401.23
 8   Jolly      254.34     245.45     245.45     354.46     245.32
 9   Magnini    234.54     342.44     267.23     242.61     265.78
10   Nguyen     264.34     434.56     278.54     367.43     345.61
11   ------------------------------------------------------------------------------------
12   Totals     1633.75
13   Averages   272.2916
14   High       345.65
15   Low        234.54
16   ------------------------------------------------------------------------------------
```

- Change the Global Format for values to the Fixed Format with 2 decimal places.
- Copy the formula in cell G5 into cells G6 to G10.
- Copy the formula in cell H5 into cells H6 to H10.
- Copy the formulas in cells B12 to B15 into cells C12 to F15.
- Print one copy of the report.

EXERCISE 9

Moving Text and Values and Deleting Columns

- Enter the following information in columns A to G as shown below. (Option: Retrieve file <u>EXER9</u>.)

	A	B	C	D	E	F	G	H
1	Payroll Record							
2	==							
3		Name	Regular		Overtime			
4			Hours		Hours	Age	Sex	
5		--						
6		Cole, B.	40		3	36	Male	
7		Dole, R.	38		0	19	Female	
8		Evers, T.	36		0	24	Female	
9		Fults, D.	40		0	58	Male	
10		Getz, W.	40		6	34	Female	
11		Robb, N.	40		6	23	Male	
12		Smith, G.	37		0	27	Male	
13		Topps, A.	40		0	52	Male	
14		Unzer, N.	40		4	31	Female	

- Notice that entries are not included in columns A and D.
- Move the information in column B to column A (beginning with row 3).
- Delete column B.
- Delete column C, which is now empty.
- Move the heading (Name) from cell A3 to cell A4.
- Print one copy of the report.

EXERCISE 10 Inserting and Deleting Rows

OVERVIEW OF BASICS

- Enter the following information in columns A to G as shown below. (Option: Retrieve file <u>EXER10</u>.)

```
       A        B        C        D        E        F        G        H
 1  Class Roll
 2  ===============================================================
 3  Name      Sex      Test 1   Test 2   Test 3   Test 4   Average
 4  ---------------------------------------------------------------
 5  Abbot, B.          67       72       75       69
 6  Dong, L.           87       93       85       97
 7  Ebbs, M.           96       93       89       93
 8  Foote, V.          65       58       63       69
 9  Gault, W.          78       73       81       79
10  Hall, R.           92       88       95       89
11  Isele, A.          52       67       66       73
12  Malik, C.          98       86       86       95
13  ---------------------------------------------------------------
14  Average
15  ===============================================================
```

- Delete column B. (See instructions in Exercise 9, if needed.)
- Delete the row containing the name: Hall, R.
- Insert a blank row "after" the name: Ebbs, M.
- Enter the following information on the blank row:
  Flood, C.   98   93   94   92
- In the space below write the formulas needed in cell F5 and cell B14 to compute the average for Abbot, B. and Test 1.

  F5 _____   B14 _____
- Enter the formulas in the worksheet.
- Copy the formula in cell F5 into cells F6 to F12.
- Copy the formula in cell B14 into cells C14 to F14.
- Format all cells containing averages for Fixed Format with 2 decimal places.
- Print one copy of the report.

EXERCISE 11   Inserting Columns

- Enter the following information in columns A to F as shown below. (Option: Retrieve file EXER11.)

```
        A         B        C         D         E         F        G         H
1   Class Roll
2   =============================================================
3   Name      Test 1   Test 2   Test 3   Test 4   Average
4   -------------------------------------------------------------
5   Abbot, B.    67       72       75       69      70.75
6   Dong, L.     87       93       85       97      90.50
7   Ebbs, M.     96       93       89       93      92.75
8   Flood, C.    98       93       94       92      94.25
9   Foote, V.    65       58       63       69      63.75
10  Gault, W.    78       73       81       79      77.75
11  Isele, A.    52       67       66       73      64.50
12  Malik, C.    98       86       86       95      91.25
13  -------------------------------------------------------------
14  Average   80.13    79.38    79.88    83.38    80.69
15  =============================================================
```

- Insert a blank column "after' the Test 2 column (column C).
- Enter Midterm as the "column D" heading. Add appropriate rulings.
- Add the following Midterm scores beginning in cell D5:
    87   89   84   65   75   91   68   74
- In the space below write the functional formula needed to compute the Average Midterm score.

    D14 _____

- Enter the formula in the worksheet.
- Format cell D14 appropriately.
- Print one copy of the report.

OVERVIEW OF BASICS

EXERCISE 12

Providing a Label Prefix

- Enter the following information in columns A to G as shown below. (Option: Retrieve file EXER12.)

```
        A        B         C        D         E        F         G         H
 1  Interest Computation
 2
 3  ============================================================================
 4  Name     Phone     ID No.   Loan      Rate     Years    Interest
 5  ----------------------------------------------------------------------------
 6  Betz, M. 555-2854 218P       3600      0.08      12
 7  Busi, L. 555-3421 456W       3760      0.16      14
 8  Doby, L. 555-4578 321T       2456      0.12      22
 9  Hoag, W. 555-3874 405K       2956      0.11       8
10  Jobs, A. 555-1034 316U       4000      0.18       5
11  Lea, B.  555-3754 435M       6000      0.12      12
12  Nery, R. 555-7329 316Y       6200      0.15      25
13  Quin, V. 555-5481 437A       4800      0.14      15
14  ============================================================================
```

- Change label prefixes as indicated below:

  Center the headings for columns A and B.
  Center the heading and data in column C.
  Right-align the headings for columns D to G.

- In the space below write the formula needed to compute the interest amount for Betz, M. (Loan Amount × Rate × Years.)
  G6 _____

- Enter the formula in the worksheet.
- Copy the formula from cell G6 into cells G7 to G13.
- Format the interest amounts for Comma Format with 0 decimal places.
- Print one copy of the report.

EXERCISE 13

Erasing Text and Values

- Enter the following information in columns A to G as shown below. (Option: Retrieve file EXER13.)

```
       A        B          C          D          E        F          G          H
1   Payroll Record
2   ================================================================
3            Name       Regular             Overtime
4                       Hours               Hours    Age        Sex
5   ----------------------------------------------------------------
6            Cole, B.     40                   3      36 Male
7            Dole, R.     38                   0      19 Female
8            Evers, T.    36                   0      24 Female
9            Fults, D.    40                   0      58 Male
10           Getz, W.     40                   6      34 Female
11           Robb, N.     40                   6      23 Male
12           Smith, G.    37                   0      27 Male
13           Topps, A.    40                   0      52 Male
14           Unzer, N.    40                   4      31 Female
15  ================================================================
```

- Delete overtime hours for Robb, N.
- Delete the data for column F, but leave the column heading (Age).
- Delete the data for column G, but leave the column heading (Sex).
- Delete column D.
- Move all information (except for the words: Payroll Record) one column to the left.
- Print one copy of the report.

Name _____ Date _____ Section _____ Evaluation _____

EXERCISE 14   Specifying Global Formats

- Enter the following information in columns A to C as shown below. (Option: Retrieve file <u>EXER14</u>.)

	A	B	C	D	E	F	G	H
1	Value Formats							
2								
3	2783.45	14.89	189					
4	2784.45	34.44	242					
5	3624.89	87.26	394					
6	3453.44	34.21	345					
7	2332.33	34.78	383					
8	3278.22	23.21	198					
9	4389.41	34.32	592					
10	3451.31	23.23	638					
11	2984.28	28.36	672					
12	2432.25	89.26	819					

- Global Format all values for Fixed Format with 1 decimal place. View the changed format.
- Global Format all values for Comma Format with 2 decimal places. View the changed format.
- Global Format all values for Currency Format with 0 decimal places. View the changed format.
- Print one copy of the final worksheet after the last format change has been made.

OVERVIEW OF BASICS

EXERCISE 15

Providing Range Names

- Enter the following information in columns A to E as shown below. (Option: Retrieve file <u>EXER15</u>.)

```
           A          B          C          D          E          F
1   Checkbook Analysis
2   ===========================================================
3   Item       Dobbs      Maxwell    Penn       Rosetti
4   -----------------------------------------------------------
5   Balance     2894.28    1342.98    7624.13    1468.29
6   Checks       348.36    1782.96    2356.45     782.19
7   Deposits     209.24    1876.45    2892.67     732.41
8   -----------------------------------------------------------
9   Balance
10  ===========================================================
```

- In the space below write the formula needed to compute the balance for Dobbs.

  B9 _____

- Enter the formula in the worksheet.
- Copy the formula from cell B9 into cells C9 to E9.
- Assign the following range names: ONE for cells B5 to B9, TWO for cells C5 to C9, THREE for cells D5 to D9, and FOUR for cells E5 to E9.
- Use range names to format ONE for Fixed Format with 1 decimal place, TWO for Comma Format with 2 decimal places, THREE for Currency Format with 2 decimal places, and FOUR for Currency Format with 2 decimal places.
- Print one copy of the formatted worksheet.

Name _____ Date _____ Section _____ Evaluation _____

EXERCISE 16 Using Parenthesis Hierarchy

- Enter the following information in columns A to D as shown below. (Option: Retrieve file <u>EXER16</u>.)

	A	B	C	D	E	F
1	Computation Hierarchy					
2						
3	13.45	16.4	34.2	32.4		
4	78.16	12.8	23.1	34.4		
5	92.14	23.4	56.3	76.5		
6	45.67	12.6	23.3	23.4		
7	12.34	15.7	21.4	21.4		
8	14.34	21.5	23.4	45.7		

- Format cells E3 to E8 for Fixed Format with 1 decimal place.
- In the spaces below write the formulas needed to perform the following computations in column E.

COMPUTATION	FORMULA
Divide the sum of cells A3 and B3 by the sum of cells C3 and D3.	E3 _____
Multiply the sum of cells A4 and C4 by 3.43.	E4 _____
Compute the square root of the sum of cells A5 and C5.	E5 _____
Raise the sum of cells A6 and D6 to the second power.	E6 _____
Divide the sum of cells A7, B7, and C7 by the sum of cell D7 and 4.	E7 _____
Add the product of cells A8 and B8 to the sum of cells C8 and D8 times 8.35.	E8 _____

- Enter the six formulas in the worksheet.
- Print one copy of the report.

EXERCISE 17 Integrated Reinforcement

- Enter the following information in columns A to E as shown below. Note: Values for this exercise are not stored on the disk. The only entries to be made in column D are the rulings.

```
        A          B          C          D          E          F          G          H
 1  Integrated Reinforcement - Overview of Basics
 2  ================================================
 3             Hours      Pay                   Gross
 4  ID No.     Worked     Rate                  Pay
 5  -----------------------------------------------
 6  243-33        40       7.89
 7  312-77        40       7.46
 8  918-45        37      10.76
 9  278-62        28      12.75
10  786-27        40       9.37
11  -----------------------------------------------
12  Average
13  High
14  Low
15  Total
16  ================================================
```

- Enter the formula to compute Gross Pay in cell E6. Copy the formula into cells E7 to E10.
- Enter the appropriate formulas in cells B12 to B15. Copy the formulas to cells C12 to E15. Note: Ignore the ERR message in column D.
- Delete column D.
- Format the "new" column D for Fixed Format with 2 decimal places.
- Format cells C12 to C15 for Fixed Format with 2 decimal places.
- Format cell D15 for Comma Format with 2 decimal places.
- Print one copy of the worksheet.

EXERCISE 18 Setting Decimal Places and Formats

• Enter the following information in columns A to F as shown below. (Option: Retrieve file EXER18.)

	A	B	C	D	E	F	G	H
1	Monthly Rental Income							
2	===							
3	Unit	Month	Month	Month	Month	Total		
4	Number	One	Two	Three	Four	Rent		
5	---							
6		1	528.7	528.7	538.6	548.6		
7		2	829.5	829.5	870.4	870.4		
8		3	672.6	685.7	685.7	690.2		
9		4	785.8	790.5	790.5	790.5		
10	---							
11	Total:							
12	Mean:							
13	High:							
14	Low:							
15	Total Amount for All Properties:							
16	===							

• Use the Global Format to display all values in the Fixed Format with 2 decimal places. View the worksheet.
• Format column A for Fixed Format with 0 decimal places.
• Format column F for Comma Format with 2 decimal places.
• Format cell E11 for Fixed Format with 2 decimal places.
• In the space below write the formula needed to compute the total rent for Unit No. 1.

F6 _____

• Enter the formula in the worksheet. Copy the formula from cell F6 into cells F7 to F9.
• Enter appropriate formulas for cells B11 to B14. Copy these formulas into cells C11 to F14.
• In the space below write the formula needed to compute total rent due from all properties.

F15 _____

• Enter the formula in the worksheet.
• Print one copy of the report.

EXERCISE 19 Creating Memorandums

- Enter the following text material as shown below. IMPORTANT: All of the text for each row is entered in the first column of the row. (Option: Retrieve file EXER19.)

```
        A       B       C       D       E       F       G       H
1   TO ALL EMPLOYEES:
2
3   Congratulations to each of you for a job well done!
4   Your efforts have helped us to exceed our annual
5   sales quota by over $100,000.  Based on this record sales report,
6   each of you will be eligible for a $500 bonus check which will
7   be distributed within 15 days after the end of the month.
8
```

- Widen column A to 40 spaces to provide a 40-space line for the text that will be placed in the column (see below).
- Justify the text in column A so that it will appear as text material in the column. After justification, the text should appear as shown below:

```
                    A                       B       C       D
1   TO ALL EMPLOYEES:
2
3   Congratulations to each of you for a job
4   well done! Your efforts have helped us
5   to exceed our annual sales quota by over
6   $100,000.  Based on this record sales
7   report, each of you will be eligible for
8   a $500 bonus check which will be
9   distributed within 15 days after the end
10  of the month.
```

- Print one copy of the worksheet.

19

EXERCISE 20 Changing Text Alignment and Formats

- Enter the following information in columns A to F as shown below. (Option: Retrieve file EXER20.)

```
         A        B        C         D        E        F        G        H
 1  Payroll File
 2  ================================================================
 3                        Birth    Current   Merit    Future
 4  Name        Sex       Year     Salary    Raise    Salary
 5  ----------------------------------------------------------------
 6  Abbot, P.M            1956     28426     0.07
 7  Dove, C.  M           1969     29528     0.12
 8  Dunn, P.  F           1962     37892     0.15
 9  Gunn, T.  M           1973     19787     0.09
10  Hall, D.  F           1962     25632     0.11
11  Pugh, R.  F           1961     35765     0.12
12  Roe, G.   M           1972     38519     0.05
13  ================================================================
```

- In the space below, write the formula needed to compute the future salary for Abbot, P.

  F6 _____

- Enter the formula in the worksheet and then copy it into cells F7 to F12.
- Use the range command to change label prefixes as follows:

  Center cell A4.
  Center cells B4 to B12. Then add the ruling back to cell B5.
  Right-align cells C3 to F4.

- Format cells D6 to D12 for Comma Format with 0 decimal places.
- Format cells E6 to E12 for Percent Format with 0 decimal places.
- Format cells F6 to F12 for Comma Format with 0 decimal places.
- Print one copy of the worksheet.

EXERCISE 21 Changing Column Widths

- Enter the following information in columns A to E as shown below. Widen column widths as needed to display the information attractively. (Note: Values for this exercise are not stored on disk.)

```
            A                    B              C          D     E
1   Address Listing
2   ================================================================
3   Name                Street         City          State ZIP
4   ----------------------------------------------------------------
5   Breymeirer, John A.  201 Forbes     Annapolis      MD    21401
6   Campora, Andy J.     230 Ashmont    Boston         MA    02189
7   Chron, Vera Anne     238 Norwood Ave Atlanta       GA    30317
8   Flaherty, Bobby K.   1601 N. Myrtle Jacksonville   FL    32209
9   Horowitz, Brian P.   346 Kingston   Detroit        MI    48237
10  Lopez, Adelaida      9300 Cady Ave  Omaha          NE    68534
11  Moore, Nancy T.      1821 Evarts    Philadelphia   PA    19252
12  Schruggs, Felecia G. 1800 Wisdom Dr Amarillo       TX    79106
13  Stokes, Jeffrey W.   216 Cape Charles Arlington    VA    23310
14  Wooten, LaSheria     398 Big Pine   Beverly Hills  CA    93613
15  Yancey, Claudette R. 610 Washington Kansas City    MO    64105
```

- Print one copy of the report.

APPEARANCE OF REPORTS

EXERCISE 22   Printing Headers

- Enter the following information in columns A to E as shown below. (Option: Retrieve file EXER22.)

	A	B	C	D	E	F
1	Attorney Client List					
2	===					
3		Phone	Hours	Pay	Amount	
4	Name	No.	Worked	Rate	Due	
5	--					
6	Amini, Mohammad	555-2376	37	75		
7	Campbell, Charles	555-2863	14	95		
8	Capote, Henry C.	555-3873	23	75		
9	Delishi, Carole A.	555-3818	21	75		
10	Gonzales, Carlos M.	555-8712	34	75		
11	Jackson, Wade C.	555-0183	75	95		
12	Nath, Ravi	555-3917	34	75		
13	Palvia, Prashant	555-4323	12	75		
14	Satterfield, Don	555-0182	18	75		
15	Schooley, Robert	555-7849	24	95		
16	Simon, Judith	555-3714	42	95		
17	Williams, Roy	555-3712	22	75		
18	===					

- Change the width of column A to 23 spaces.
- In the space below write the formula needed to compute the amount due for Amini, Mohammad.

  E6 _____

- Enter the formula in the worksheet. Then copy the formula into cells E7 to E17.
- Format the data in column E for Comma Format with 0 decimal places.
- Right-align cells C3 to E4.
- Center cells A3 to B4.
- Print the report with the following header: Confidential (Note: Use menus and prompts to make the above notation print at the top of the worksheet.)

EXERCISE 23 Printing Footers

- Enter the following information in columns A to E as shown below. (Option: Retrieve file EXER23.)

```
               A              B         C        D        E        F
 1  Attorney Client List
 2  ===================================================================
 3                          Phone     Hours     Pay     Amount
 4          Name            No.       Worked    Rate     Due
 5  -------------------------------------------------------------------
 6  Amini, Mohammad         555-2376    37        75     2,775
 7  Campbell, Charles       555-2863    14        95     1,330
 8  Capote, Henry C.        555-3873    23        75     1,725
 9  Delishi, Carole A.      555-3818    21        75     1,575
10  Gonzales, Carlos M.     555-8712    34        75     2,550
11  Jackson, Wade C.        555-0183    75        95     7,125
12  Nath, Ravi              555-3917    34        75     2,550
13  Palvia, Prashant        555-4323    12        75       900
14  Satterfield, Don        555-0182    18        75     1,350
15  Schooley, Robert        555-7849    24        95     2,280
16  Simon, Judith           555-3714    42        95     3,990
17  Williams, Roy           555-3712    22        75     1,650
18  ===================================================================
```

- Print one copy of the report with the following footer: Return to Room 2186. Also, include a header that prints the page number.

EXERCISE 24   Printing Borders

- Enter the following information in columns A to F as shown below. (Option: Retrieve file EXER24.)

	A	B	C	D	E	F	G
1	O	Attorney Client List					
2	V	==					
3	E		Phone	Hours	Pay	Amount	
4	R	Name	No.	Worked	Rate	Due	
5	D	--					
6	U	Amini, Mohammad	555-2376	37	75	2,775	
7	E	Campbell, Charles	555-2863	14	95	1,330	
8		Capote, Henry C.	555-3873	23	75	1,725	
9	A	Delishi, Carole A.	555-3818	21	75	1,575	
10	C	Gonzales, Carlos M.	555-8712	34	75	2,550	
11	C	Jackson, Wade C.	555-0183	75	95	7,125	
12	O	Nath, Ravi	555-3917	34	75	2,550	
13	U	Palvia, Prashant	555-4323	12	75	900	
14	N	Satterfield, Don	555-0182	18	75	1,350	
15	T	Schooley, Robert	555-7849	24	95	2,280	
16	S	Simon, Judith	555-3714	42	95	3,990	
17		Williams, Roy	555-3712	22	75	1,650	
18		==					

- Print one copy of the report with the following border: OVERDUE ACCOUNTS

EXERCISE 25

Printing Cell Formulas

- Enter the following information in columns A to E as shown below. (Option: Retrieve file <u>EXER25</u>.)

```
          A            B           C          D            E          F
 1  Loan Report
 2  ==========================================================
 3  No.        Principal     Rate      Time (Days)    Interest
 4  ----------------------------------------------------------
 5  128Q            1280      0.08          180
 6  129Q            2760      0.125         365
 7  130Q            3600      0.09          720
 8  131Q            4200      0.145          90
 9  132Q            1800      0.12          240
10  133Q            2400      0.105         185
11  134Q           12000      0.125         180
12  135Q            9600      0.115         180
13  136Q            2400      0.125         120
14  ----------------------------------------------------------
15                                         Total:
16                                         Average:
17  ==========================================================
```

- Enter the formula needed to compute interest amounts (based on 365 days in a year) in cell E5. Then copy the formula from cell E5 into cells E6 to E13.
- Enter the formulas needed to compute total interest amount and average interest amount in cells E15 and E16 respectively.
- Format values in column B for the Comma Format with 0 decimal places.
- Format values in column C for Percent Format with 1 decimal place.
- Format <u>all</u> values in column E for the Comma Format with 2 decimal places.
- Right-align cells B3 to E3.
- Print one copy of the report.
- Print one copy of the cell formulas <u>only</u>.

25

EXERCISE 26

Changing Margins and Using Data Fill

- Enter the following information in columns A to F as shown below. (Option: Retrieve file <u>EXER26</u>.)

```
         A            B              C        D        E       F        G
1   Monthly Rental Cash Flow
2   =============================================================
3                             PITI      Repair   Rental   Cash
4   No.        Property       Payments  Expenses Income   Flow
5   -------------------------------------------------------------
6              1836 Elm Street   489.53   162.5    585
7              2463 Davies Dr    628.76    15      720
8              2762 Brad Blvd    568.24   78.64    650
9              1504 Birch Rd     789.55   75       925
10             7905 Water Leaf   752.92  125.63    975
11             5462 DeLoach      504.16   57.25    795
12             1508 Quince       306.21   25       525
13             814 Watson        380.36   79.16    450
14  =============================================================
```

- Use Data Fill in cells A6 to A13 to number the properties consecutively, beginning with the value 1 in cell A6.
- Use Global Format to format all values for Fixed Format with 2 decimal places.
- Use Range format to format values in column A for Fixed Format with 0 decimal places.
- In the space below write the formula needed to compute Cash Flow for No. 1.

  F6 _____

- Enter the formula in the worksheet. Then copy it into cells F7 to F13.
- Print one copy of the worksheet.
- Delete columns C to F.
- Print one copy of the revised report with a left margin of 20 spaces.

EXERCISE 27 Protecting Cell Contents

- Enter the following information in columns A to D as shown below. (Option: Retrieve file EXER27.)

```
          A           B          C          D          E          F          G
 1   Auto Inventory Report
 2   ================================================
 3   Vehicle     Lot        Days on    Days to
 4   ID          Location   Lot        Shipment
 5   ------------------------------------------------
 6   42L89Q      South           17          8
 7   89V24P      North           23         12
 8   76L72S      South           18         17
 9   14V53Q      West            19          9
10   71P81T      North           17         15
11   54N73A      East            15         21
12   76B81R      West            18         12
13   ------------------------------------------------
14   Average
15   ================================================
```

- Right-align cells C3 to D4.
- Enter formulas in cells C14 and D14 to compute the averages for columns C and D respectively.
- Protect cells C14 and D14 so that entries cannot be made in these cells.
- Try to make entries in these two cells. (Note: You should hear a "beep" and be unable to make entries in these protected cells.)
- Print one copy of the report.

APPEARANCE OF REPORTS

EXERCISE 28   Integrated Reinforcement

APPEARANCE OF REPORTS

- Enter the following information in columns A to E as shown below. (Option: Retrieve file <u>EXER28</u>.)

```
             A           B        C      D     E      F        G        H
 1  Attorney Client List
 2  =========================================
 3                    Phone    Hours Pay Amount
 4  Name              No.      WorkedRateDue
 5  ----------------------------------------
 6  Allen, Alice      555-3873   23  75 1725
 7  Brown, Judy       555-2863   14  95 1330
 8  Feldman, Jesse    555-0183   75  95 7125
 9  Mehra, Satish     555-2376   37  75 2775
10  Meyer, Ann        555-0182   18  75 1350
11  Pracht, William555-8712      34  75 2550
12  Wilkes, Ronnie    555-3917   34  75 2550
13  Wills, Cliff      555-3818   21  75 1575
14  Zeltmann, Steve555-4323      12  75  900
15  =========================================
```

- Change each column width as needed to make the report more attractive.
- Center cell A4.
- Right-align cells B3 to E4.
- Format the values in column E for the Comma Format with 0 decimal places.
- Protect cells E6 to E14.
- Try to make an entry in one of these protected cells (E6 to E14). Notice that a "beep" sounds and you are unable to make the entry in the cell.
- Prepare a "header" to number the page.
- Print one copy of the report with a left margin of 8 spaces.

EXERCISE 29 Using @DATE

- Enter the following information in columns A to D as shown below. (Option: Retrieve file <u>EXER29</u>.)

```
            A           B           C           D         E         F         G
1   Marketing Sales Quotas
2   =======================================
3   Current Date:
4   ---------------------------------------
5                   Current               Percent
6   Date            Quota       Sales     Change
7   ---------------------------------------
8                    7500        7675
9                    7600        7915
10                   7500        7385
11                   7500        7763
12                   7800        7955
13                   7600        7975
14                   7500        7345
15                   7700        7936
16  =======================================
```

- Enter @DATE format—@DATE (Year-Number, Month-Number, Day-Number)—for April 12, 1989, in cell C3.
- Enter the @DATE format for April 3, 1990, in cell A8.
- Enter the @DATE format for April 4, 1990, in cell A9.
- Continue with the @DATE format for consecutive dates in cells A10 to A15.
- Format cell C3 for the Date Format (DD-MMM-YY).
- Format cells A8 to A15 for the Date Format (DD-MMM-YY).
- Enter the formula in cell D8 to compute the Percent Change.
- Copy the formula in cell D8 into cells D9 to D15.
- Format cells D8 to D15 for the Percent Format with 1 decimal place.
- Print one copy of the report.

29

EXERCISE 30   Using DATE Arithmetic

- Enter the following information in columns A to E as shown below. Change column widths as needed. (Option: Retrieve file UNDERLINE EXER30.)

	A	B	C	D	E	F
1	Bond Maturity Date Schedule					
2	==					
3	Bond	Maturity	Origination	Days to	Maturity	
4	No.	Value	Date	Maturity	Date	
5	--					
6	P3453	42,000		3650		
7	T4232	36,000		7620		
8	Y4382	34,000		3650		
9	N5824	32,000		2825		
10	B3492	64,000		3620		
11	P4839	32,000		3433		
12	E3481	97,500		8430		
13	E3892	48,200		3750		
14	T4534	56,500		4000		
15	==					

- Use the @DATE format to enter the following dates in cells C6 to C14 (Origination Date column).

  C6   November 23, 1987 (Note: Enter as @DATE(87,11,23))
  C7   August 20, 1977
  C8   January 3, 1987
  C9   September 30, 1989
  C10 March 24, 1989
  C11 August 20, 1987
  C12 April 22, 1976
  C13 August 21, 1989
  C14 September 9, 1985

- Format cells C6 to C14 for the Date Format: @DATE(DD-MMM-YY)
- In the space below write the formula needed to add the "Days to Maturity" to the "Origination Date" for the first bond.

  E6 _____

- Enter the formula in the worksheet.
- Copy the formula from cell E6 into cells E7 to E14.
- Format cells E6 to E14 for the Date Format (DD-MMM-YY).
- Print one copy of the worksheet.

EXERCISE 31 Finding the Remainder

- Enter the following information in columns A to D as shown below. (Option: Retrieve file EXER31.)

```
      A          B         C          D        E      F      G
1  Product Distribution
2  =======================================
3     Item     Total     Total      Items
4    Number    Items     Stores   Remaining
5  ---------------------------------------
6  P209        2,465      189
7  R234       12,763      198
8  U786        9,825      176
9  P492       23,871      189
10 P487       19,473      189
11 P473       37,249      176
12 =======================================
```

- Use the @MOD functional formula to determine the number of items that will remain if an even number of each item is shipped to each store.
- Print one copy of the worksheet.

EXERCISE 32   Converting to Integer Values

FUNCTION: MATHEMATICAL

- Enter the following information in columns A to D as shown below. (Option: Retrieve file <u>EXER32</u>.)

	A	B	C	D	E	F	G	H
1	Finding the Integer Part of a Number							
2	====================================							
3	No. 1	No. 2	No. 3	No. 4				
4	------------------------------------							
5	365.894	45.3246	987.92	763.385				
6	453.89	276.3217	762.7834	879.43				
7	789.45	451.54	981.6	784.54				
8	346.78	345.21	981.4	893.329				
9	====================================							
10								
11								
12								
13								
14	====================================							

- In the space below write the functional formula needed to convert the value in cell A5 to a corresponding integer value in cell A10.

    A10 _____

- Enter the formula in the worksheet.
- Copy the formula from cell A10 into cells A11 to A13.
- Copy the formulas from cells A10 to A13 to the following range: cells B10 to D13.
- Print one copy of the worksheet.

EXERCISE 33   Finding the Highest and Lowest Value

- Enter the following information in columns A and B as shown below, with values formatted for currency and 2 decimal places. Widen columns as needed. (Option: Retrieve file EXER33.)

```
                A                    B            C        D        E
1   Weekly Sales Report for April
2   =====================================
3   Salesperson             April
4   ------------------------------------
5   Abbott, John A.         $23,465.35
6   Carlson, Maria T.       $18,432.89
7   Fortenberry, Joan A.    $24,534.89
8   Getz, Robert R.         $29,781.54
9   Jenzen, Carla E.        $27,543.98
10  Mooney, Paula F.        $23,599.99
11  ------------------------------------
12  Highest Sale:
13  ------------------------------------
14  Lowest Sale:
15  =====================================
```

- In the space below write the functional formula needed in cell B12 to compute the highest sales amount. Also, write the functional formula needed in cell B14 to compute the lowest sales amount for April.

   B12 _____   B14 _____

- Enter the formulas in the worksheet.
- Print one copy of the worksheet.

33

EXERCISE 34   Counting Values

- Enter the following information in columns A and B as shown below. (Options: Retrieve file <u>EXER34</u> or the file saved in Exercise 33.)

```
            A                    B          C        D        E
 1  Weekly Sales Report for April
 2  ==================================
 3  Salesperson          April
 4  ----------------------------------
 5  Abbott, John A.      $23,465.35
 6  Carlson, Maria T.    $18,432.89
 7  Fortenberry, Joan A. $24,534.89
 8  Getz, Robert R.      $29,781.54
 9  Jenzen, Carla E.     $27,543.98
10  Mooney, Paula F.     $23,599.99
11  ----------------------------------
12  Highest Sale:        $29,781.54
13  ----------------------------------
14  Lowest Sale:         $18,432.89
15  ==================================
16  No. of Salespeople:
17  ==================================
```

- In the space below write the functional formula needed in cell B16 to compute the number of salespeople included in the report.
  B16 _____
- Enter the formula in the worksheet. Format cell B16 for Fixed Format with 0 decimal places.
- Print one copy of the worksheet.

34

EXERCISE 35   Computing Totals

FUNCTION: MATHEMATICAL

- Enter the following information in columns A and B as shown below. (Option: Retrieve file <u>EXER35</u>.)

```
            A                      B            C        D        E
1   Weekly Sales Report for April
2   =======================================
3        Salesperson          April
4   ---------------------------------------
5   Abbott, John A.           $23,465.35
6   Carlson, Maria T.         $18,432.89
7   Fortenberry, Joan A.      $24,534.89
8   Getz, Robert R.           $29,781.54
9   Jenzen, Carla E.          $27,543.98
10  Mooney, Paula F.          $23,599.99
11  ---------------------------------------
12  Total Sales:
13  =======================================
```

- In the space below write the functional formula needed in cell B12 to compute the total sales for the month.

  B12 _____
- Enter the formula in the worksheet. Use an appropriate format for the total.
- Print one copy of the worksheet.

Name _____ Date _____ Section _____ Evaluation _____

EXERCISE 36 Computing Averages

- Enter the following information in columns A and B as shown below. (Option: Retrieve file EXER36.)

```
      A         B        C        D        E        F        G        H
1  Basketball Team Averages
2  ==================
3  Team      Points
4  ------------------
5  Bullets      114
6  Bulls        108
7  Celtics      117
8  Hawks         99
9  Hornets       97
10 Jazz         103
11 Lakers       115
12 Pistons      112
13 Spurs         96
14 ------------------
15 Average:
16 ==================
17 Highest:
18 ==================
19 Lowest:
20 ==================
```

- In the space below write the functional formula needed in cell B15 to compute the average number of points scored.

  B15 _____

- Enter the formula in the worksheet. Also, enter appropriate formulas in cells B17 and B19. Format cell B15 for 2 decimal places.
- Print one copy of the worksheet.

EXERCISE 37 Computing Periodic Payments

- Enter the following information in columns A to E as shown below. Provide appropriate column widths and value formats. (Option: Retrieve file EXER37.)

```
         A              B           C            D          E
1   Monthly Loan Payments
2   ==========================================================
3                     Amount    Interest    Repayment  Monthly
4        Item        Financed     Rate    Period (Months) Payment
5   ----------------------------------------------------------
6   Auto              14,500     12.5%          48
7   Boat               4,800     14.5%          24
8   House            128,400     12.0%         360
9   Fur Coat           7,600     16.5%          30
10  Television           899     14.5%          18
11  Refrigerator         719     14.5%          24
12  Auto              14,780     14.5%          60
13  House             13,876     12.5%         180
14  Jewelry            5,200     14.5%          24
15  ----------------------------------------------------------
16  Total Monthly Payments:
17  ==========================================================
```

- In the space below write the functional formula needed in cell E6 to compute the periodic payment needed to retire the loan for the auto.

  E6 _____

- Enter the formula in the worksheet. Copy the formula from cell E6 into cells E7 to E14. Format values in column E for 2 decimal places.
- Enter the functional formula needed in cell E16 to compute the total monthly payments.
- Print one copy of the worksheet.
- Experiment by changing various loan amounts financed, interest rates, and months needed to pay the loan amount. Notice that the monthly payment needed for the loan will automatically be computed each time an entry is made.

EXERCISE 38 Computing Net Present Value

- Enter the following information in columns A to C as shown below. (Option: Retrieve file EXER38.)

```
           A                              B              C              D
1   Net Present Value of an Investment
2   ==================================================================
3    Current Investment Amount:        $100,000       $72,500
4   ------------------------------------------------------------------
5        Year 1 Expected Income:        $25,000       $15,000
6        Year 2 Expected Income:        $25,000       $16,000
7        Year 3 Expected Income:        $25,000       $17,500
8        Year 4 Expected Income:        $25,000       $18,000
9        Year 5 Expected Income:        $25,000       $18,000
10  ------------------------------------------------------------------
11       Estimated Interest Rate:        12.0%          9.5%
12  ------------------------------------------------------------------
13           Net Present Value:
14  ------------------------------------------------------------------
```

- Problem: John Dill has an opportunity to receive $25,000 during each of the next five years or $100,000 today. You will use the worksheet to compute the net present value of the $25,000 cash flow income, assuming that the estimated interest rate is 12.0 percent.
- In the space below write the formula needed to compute the net present value amount of the cash flow ($25,000 for each year) for the five years.
  B13 _____
- Enter the formula in the worksheet.
- Enter the functional formula in cell C13 to compute the net present value of the second investment.
- Which option appears to be the best one for John Dill?

  _____

  A. $100,000 today

  B. $25,000 each year for the next five years
- Print one copy of the worksheet.
- Change the estimated interest rate to 5.0 percent (0.05) in cell B11. View the screen. Based on this interest rate, which of the above options appears to be the best one for John Dill? _____

Name _____ Date _____ Section _____ Evaluation _____

EXERCISE 39   Computing Internal Rate of Return

- Enter the following information in columns A to D as shown below. (Option: Retrieve file EXER39.)

```
             A                      B           C           D
1   Internal Rate of Return on Investments
2   =========================================================
3                              Conway Stock  TMX Stock   CHX Stock
4                              ------------------------------------
5        Initial Investment:    ($8,000)    ($8,000)    ($8,000)
6    Year 1 Dividend Income:      $350        $125        $100
7    Year 2 Dividend Income:      $275         $95        $100
8    Year 3 Dividend Income:      $275        $115        $125
9    Year 4 Dividend Income:      $295        $105         $95
10     Year 5 Sales Amount:      $8,400      $8,500      $8,600
11                             ------------------------------------
12  Internal Rate of Return:
13                             ------------------------------------
```

- Notice that the initial investment amount (row 5) is included in the range as a negative cash flow since this amount must be provided at the beginning of the first year and that the sales price amount is also included in the range since this amount will be received as a positive cash flow.
- Problem: Carol Beltz decides to invest $8,000 in each of three investments. The investments will earn various dividend amounts each year and will have various sales amounts when sold as shown in the above worksheet template. Assume that the estimated interest rate is 8.5 percent for each investment. Compute the internal rate of return for each investment.
- In the space below write the @IRR functional formula needed in cell B12 to compute the internal rate of return for the first investment. Format cells B12 to D12 for Percent Format with 2 decimal places.

  B12 _____

- Enter the formula in the worksheet. Copy the formula in cell B12 into cells C12 to D12.
- Print one copy of the worksheet.
- Which of the following investments gave Carol Beltz the best rate of return on her investment? _____

  A. Conway Stock
  B. TMX Stock
  C. CHX Stock

39

EXERCISE 40 Computing Future Value of an Annuity

- Enter the following information in columns A to D as shown below. (Option: Retrieve file <u>EXER40</u>.)

```
        A           B           C         D         E      F      G
1   Future Value of an Investment
2   ==================================================
3          Monthly Interest      No. of    Future
4        Investment     Rate      Years     Value
5   --------------------------------------------------
6            $250        9.5%        18
7            $275        9.5%        18
8            $100       12.0%         5
9          $1,250       10.0%         8
10           $950       12.5%        10
11           $950       12.5%        20
12  ==================================================
```

- Problem: David and Betty Fogelman decide to invest $250 per month to save for their son's college education expenses. They will invest for 18 years with the funds earning an interest rate of 9.5 percent. Use the worksheet and the @FV functional formula to compute the amount that will accumulate after 18 years.
- In the space below write the functional formula needed to determine the above information.

  D6 _____

- Enter the formula in the worksheet.
- Copy the formula from cell D6 into cells D7 to D11 to compute the accumulated values for the remaining investments.
- Print one copy of the worksheet.
- Change the amount invested by the Fogelman family in cell A6 to $400. View the monitor to determine the amount accumulated.
- Move the cell pointer to cell A15. Don Drombrowski decides to invest $30 per month for 2 years at a 10 percent interest rate. Enter the @FV functional formula in cell A15 to compute the amount that will accumulate after 2 years. What is the amount?

  _____

EXERCISE 41

Computing Present Value of an Annuity

- Enter the following information in columns A to D as shown below. (Option: Retrieve file EXER41.)

	A	B	C	D	E	F	G
1	Present Value of Investments						
2	===						
3	Monthly	No. of	Interest	Present			
4	Income	Years	Rate	Value			
5	---						
6	$780	8	9.5%				
7	$1,200	20	10.0%				
8	$950	30	12.0%				
9	$1,500	10	10.5%				
10	$850	15	12.5%				
11	$900	15	9.5%				
12	===						

- Problem: Juan Perez inherited an investment that will pay him $780 per month for 8 years. Use the worksheet to compute the present value of the investment if the interest rate is 9.5 percent.
- In the space below write the formula needed to determine the present value of Juan's inheritance.

  D6 _____

- Enter the formula in the worksheet. Copy the formula from cell D6 into cells D7 to D11 to compute the present values for the other annuities. Format column D for Currency Format with 2 decimal places.
- Print one copy of the worksheet.
- Move the cell pointer to cell A16. Enter the @PV functional formula needed to compute the present value of an annuity of $300 per month for 15 years if the interest rate is 10.5 percent. What is the amount? _____
- Note: The difference between present value and net present value is that present value payments must be equal each period. Net present value payments do not have to be equal each period.

EXERCISE 42

Computing Variance and Standard Deviation

- Enter the following information in columns A to G as shown below. (Option: Retrieve file EXER42.)

	A	B	C	D	E	F	G
1	Test Score Statistics						
2	===						
3	Students	Test 1	Test 2	Test 3	Test 4	Average	High
4	---						
5	Carlos, Juan	67	98	89	78		
6	Darby, Bill	89	100	87	81		
7	DeGroff, James	88	80	76	53		
8	Fleming, Rose	54	67	89	92		
9	Fong, Suzy	97	52	89	47		
10	Garrett, Phillip	99	97	78	89		
11	Henson, Sabrina	69	78	89	47		
12	Issel, Saul	93	52	89	78		
13	Lowry, Paul	43	65	87	84		
14	Malone, Edward	55	73	89	97		
15	Moore, Charlie	89	84	94	68		
16	Poole, David	93	97	91	72		
17	Wertz, Guy	74	63	90	100		
18	---						

- In the space below write the formulas needed to compute the variance and standard deviation for the Test 1 scores.

  B19 _____   B20 _____

- Enter the formulas in the worksheet. Copy the formulas from B19 and B20 into cells C19 to G20.
- Enter the formulas in cells F5 and G5 needed to compute the average and high score for the first student. Copy the formulas to compute these same statistics for the remaining students.
- Format cells B19 to G20 for Fixed Format with 3 decimal places. Format cells F5 to G17 for Fixed Format with 0 decimal places.
- Print one copy of the worksheet.

EXERCISE 43

Rounding Values

- Use the @ROUND functional formula to round the following values beginning in cell A1. Note: Values for this exercise are not stored on disk.

A1	104.5636	rounded to 3 decimal places
A2	97.3891	rounded to 1 decimal place
A3	16.8934	rounded to 2 decimal places
A4	9.457	rounded to 2 decimal places
A5	10.551	rounded to 0 decimal places
A6	428.892	rounded to the nearest hundred

- Print one copy of the worksheet.

FUNCTION: MATHEMATICAL

FUNCTION: MATHEMATICAL

EXERCISE 44

Computing Square Roots

- Use the @SQRT functional formula to determine the square roots for each of the following values. Enter the values shown below in column A, beginning in cell A1. Note: Values for this exercise are not stored on disk.

A1	81
A2	1048.87
A3	1648.93
A4	7892.36
A5	893
A6	7225
A7	98473
A8	1289564

- In the space below write the formula needed to compute the square root of the first value.

  B1 _____

- Enter the formula in the worksheet. Copy the formula from cell B1 into cells B2 to B8.
- Print one copy of the worksheet.

EXERCISE 45

Determining Random Numbers

- Use the @RAND functional formula to produce a random number between 0 and 1 in cell A1. Note: Values for this exercise are not stored on disk.
- Copy the formula from cell A1 into cells A2 to A20.
- Repeat the above steps. Notice that a totally different set of random numbers was generated this time.
- Problem: Opal Gamble desires to produce a set of randomly generated numbers in a range from 0 to 100.
- Enter a formula in cell B1 that multiplies the value in cell A1 by 100. Copy the formula from cell B1 into cells B2 to B20. Format the values in column B for Fixed Format with 0 decimal places.
- Print one copy of the worksheet.

FUNCTION: MATHEMATICAL

Name _____ Date _____ Section _____ Evaluation _____

EXERCISE 46 Integrated Reinforcement

- Enter the following information in columns A to C as shown below. Enter appropriate value formats and column widths. Note: Values for this exercise are not stored on disk.

```
             A                    B              C           D
 1   Sales Report
 2   ========================================================
 3        Salesperson      Sales Amount   Random Numbers
 4   --------------------------------------------------------
 5   Abbington, Brenda        $12,423.89
 6   Baskin, Wilburn           18,549.82
 7   Carrington, Mark          13,827.84
 8   Desmond, Peter            11,873.43
 9   Gault, Anthony            17,347.23
10   Isley, Carolyn            14,392.37
11   Keller, Bobbie            12,748.89
12   --------------------------------------------------------
13              Total:
14            Average:
15   Number of Salespeople:
16        Highest Sale:
17         Lowest Sale:
18   Standard Deviation:
19   Current Date of Report:
20   ========================================================
```

- Enter the appropriate formulas in cells B13 to B19 to compute the required values. Format cells B13 to B19 for Fixed Format with 2 decimal places except for cell B15 (Fixed Format with 0 decimal places) and cell B19 (Date Format to indicate day and month only).
- Enter (and copy as needed) the formula to generate random numbers between 0 and 10 in cells C5 to C11. Then format this range for Fixed Format with 0 decimal places.
- Note: Entries will not be made in cells C13 to C19.
- Save this file as EXER47. (Note: You are saving it as EXER47 since it will be used when completing the next exercise.)
- Print one copy of the worksheet.

COPYRIGHT © 1990 BY McGRAW-HILL, INC. ALL RIGHTS RESERVED.

EXERCISE 47 Updating Files

- Retrieve file <u>EXER47</u>. The worksheet should appear as shown below.
- Change the sales amount for Peter Desmond from 11,873.43 to 19,873.43. Except for the random number generation, your worksheet should appear as shown below (prior to the change).

```
                    A                    B                 C              D
1    Sales Report
2    =======================================================
3        Salesperson         Sales Amount      Random Numbers
4    ------------------------------------------------------
5    Abbington, Brenda           $12,423.89              7
6    Baskin, Wilburn              18,549.82              9
7    Carrington, Mark             13,827.84              1
8    Desmond, Peter               11,873.43              4
9    Gault, Anthony               17,347.23              7
10   Isley, Carolyn               14,392.37              1
11   Keller, Bobbie               12,748.89              2
12   ------------------------------------------------------
13              Total:           101,163.47
14            Average:            14,451.92
15   Number of Salespeople:              7 Note:  Data in cells
16        Highest Sale:           18,549.82 C5 to C11 will vary.
17         Lowest Sale:           11,873.43
18   Standard Deviation:           2,367.35
19   Current Date of Report:         16-Oct
20   =======================================================
```

- Save the file with the same file name: <u>EXER47</u>
- Note that you will be given an indication that the file already exists. Choose the "Replace" option. The revised updated file should replace the old file on the disk.

EXERCISE 48 File List and File Erase

- Retrieve file <u>EXER47</u>. Note that the revised amount from Exercise 47 should appear in the worksheet as shown below.

```
              A                  B              C            D
1  Sales Report
2  ============================================================
3        Salesperson       Sales Amount    Random Numbers
4  ------------------------------------------------------------
5  Abbington, Brenda          $12,423.89              7
6  Baskin, Wilburn             18,549.82              8
7  Carrington, Mark            13,827.84              8
8  Desmond, Peter              19,873.43              7
9  Gault, Anthony              17,347.23              2
10 Isley, Carolyn              14,392.37              6
11 Keller, Bobbie              12,748.89              5
12 ------------------------------------------------------------
13             Total:         109,163.47
14           Average:          15,594.78
15 Number of Salespeople:              7 Note:  Data in cells
16      Highest Sale:          19,873.43 C5 to C11 will vary.
17       Lowest Sale:          12,423.89
18 Standard Deviation:          2,747.25
19 Current Date of Report:        16-Oct
20 ============================================================
```

- List your worksheet files on the screen. Note that EXER47 appears as one of the files.
- Delete the following file from the disk: EXER47
- List your worksheet files on the screen. Note that the file deleted in the previous step (EXER47) does not appear.
- Note that the worksheet still remains on the screen (and in memory) even though it has been deleted from the disk. No printed copy is required for this exercise.

EXERCISE 49 Combining Worksheets

- Enter the following information in columns A to D as shown below. Prepare appropriate column widths and value formats. (Note: Values for this exercise are not stored on disk.)

	A	B	C	D	E	F
1	Salary Projections					
2	===					
3		Current	Projected	Projected		
4	Employee	Salary	Salary	Raise		
5	---					
6	Cutler, Robert	39,750		8.5%		
7	Diaz, Juan	28,786		8.0%		
8	Fuller, Clara	32,895		8.0%		
9	Gerhard, Larry	34,672		8.5%		

- In the space below write the formula needed to compute the projected salary amount for Robert Cutler.

  C6 _____

- Enter the formula in the worksheet. Copy the formula from cell C6 into cells C7 to C9.
- Print one copy of the worksheet.
- Save the file with the following file name: A49
- Clear the screen and memory.
- Enter the following information in columns A to D as shown below. Note: Enter the formula and formulas exactly as requested for the previous worksheet shown above. Also, your column widths and formats should be identical for the two files.

	A	B	C	D	E	F
1	Huntzinger, Karl	36,489		9.5%		
2	Luttman, Glynda	42,341		7.8%		
3	Noonan, Donald	28,674		9.5%		
4	Oswalt, Beverley	33,549		8.0%		
5	Peete, Howard	38,440		9.5%		
6	Quick, Myra	46,382		9.5%		
7	Reston, Danny	32,894		9.8%		

- Save the file with the following file name: B49
- Clear the screen and memory.
- Retrieve the following file: A49
- Move the cell pointer to cell A10.
- Enter the menu commands needed to combine file B49 with file A49.
- Print one copy of the combined worksheet file.

EXERCISE 50 Freezing Titles

- Enter the following information in columns A to F as shown below. (Option: Retrieve file <u>EXER50</u>.)

```
         A        B        C          D        E        F          G
 1  Class Grade Book
 2  =================================================================
 3   Student    Test   Mid-Term     Test    Final   Overall
 4   Number     One      Exam       Two      Exam   Average
 5  -----------------------------------------------------------------
 6             1
 7             2
 8             3
 9             4
10             5
11             6
12             7
13             8
14             9
15            10
16            11
17            12
18            13
19            14
20            15
```

- Freeze the horizontal titles shown in rows 1 to 5 on the screen.
- Note that this worksheet provides space for entering four grades and a computed overall average for each student. Also, use Global Fixed Format for values, with 0 decimal places.
- In the space below write the formula needed to compute the overall average, assuming that all test scores count equally.

  F6 _____

- Enter the formula in the worksheet. Then copy the formula from cell F6 into cells F7 to F35.
- Create and enter four test scores for each of 30 students. Continue consecutive numbering in column A. Notice that the titles remain (frozen) on the screen even as you go beyond row 20.
- Print one copy of the worksheet.

EXERCISE 51 Using Multiple Windows

- Enter the information in columns A to F as shown below. Notice that columns C and D are blank. (Option: Retrieve file EXER51.)

	A	B	C	D	E	F
1	Sales Revenues					
2	========================					
3	City	Amount				
4	----------------------					
5	Atlanta	118,394			Las Vegas	176,271
6	Baltimore	129,324			Little Rock	154,365
7	Birmingham	128,321			Los Angeles	123,325
8	Boston	117,328			Louisville	112,659
9	Chicago	132,756			Memphis	139,750
10	Cincinnati	124,654			Miami	125,372
11	Columbia	145,324			Minneapolis	124,512
12	Columbus	124,923			Nashville	143,562
13	Dallas	116,734			New York	178,342
14	Denver	123,659			Orem	89,325
15	Detroit	124,541			Philadelphia	121,416
16	Georgetown	122,514			Richmond	108,783
17	Hartford	119,327			San Francisco	127,523
18	Houston	121,462			St. Louis	109,534
19	Jackson	123,326			Stillwater	101,437

- Enter the commands to freeze the titles after row 4.
- Move the information in cells E6 to F20 into cells A20 to B34.
- Change column widths as needed.
- Move the cell pointer to cell B36 and enter a formula needed to compute the total of column B.
- Move the cell pointer to cell B37 and enter the formula needed to compute the average of column B (cells B5 to B34).
- Enter the commands needed to divide the screen into two horizontal windows after row 10.
- Move the cell pointer into the bottom window and then move the cell pointer downward until both the total and average amounts appear on the screen.
- Move the cell pointer into the top window and then move the cell pointer to cell B5. Change the amount from 118,394 to 122,486. Note: Watch the total change in the bottom window as you make the change.
- Repeat the above step by moving the cell pointer to cell B8 and changing the amount from 117,328 to 136,438.
- Enter the commands needed to return the screen to one window. Then enter the commands needed to unfreeze the titles.
- Save the worksheet as file EXER51.
- Print one copy of the completed worksheet.

EXERCISE 52 Printing Page Numbers

- Retrieve the worksheet created in the previous exercise.
- The worksheet should appear as shown below.

	A	B	C	D	E	F
1	Sales Revenues					
2	=========================					
3	City	Amount				
4	-----------------------					
5	Atlanta	122,486				
6	Baltimore	129,324				
7	Birmingham	128,321				
8	Boston	136,438				
9	Chicago	132,756				
10	Cincinnati	124,654				
11	Columbia	145,324				
12	Columbus	124,923				
13	Dallas	116,734				
14	Denver	123,659				
15	Detroit	124,541				
16	Georgetown	122,514				
17	Hartford	119,327				
18	Houston	121,462				
19	Jackson	123,326				
20	Las Vegas	176,271				
21	Little Rock	154,365				
22	Los Angeles	123,325				
23	Louisville	112,659				
24	Memphis	139,750				
25	Miami	125,372				
26	Minneapolis	124,512				
27	Nashville	143,562				
28	New York	178,342				
29	Orem	89,325				
30	Philadelphia	121,416				
31	Richmond	108,783				
32	San Francisco	127,523				
33	St. Louis	109,534				
34	Stillwater	101,437				
35						
36	Total:	3,831,965				
37	Average:	127,732				

- Enter the header needed to print page numbers at the top of the page.
- Print one copy of the worksheet with page numbers.

EXERCISE 53 Using Vertical Table Lookup

- Enter the following information in columns A to C as shown below. (Option: Retrieve file EXER53.)

```
           A              B            C          D      E      F      G
1  Inventory List
2  ==========================================
3       Product         Cost        Sales
4       Number          Price       Price
5  ------------------------------------------
6        53422         673.34       823.89
7        63572         532.81       675.23
8        64327         453.89       509.29
9        79225         423.81       476.93
10       79226         727.32       835.14
11       83528         209.19       316.28
12       92734         119.34       173.22
13 ==========================================
```

- In the space below write the functional formula needed in cell A14 to use the vertical lookup feature to determine the cost price for product 64327.

  A14 _____

- Enter the formula in the worksheet.
- Enter the functional formula in cell A15 needed to determine the **cost** price for product 79226.
- Enter the functional formula in cell A16 needed to determine the **sales** price for product 53422.
- Enter the functional formula in cell A17 needed to determine the **sales** price for product 83528.
- Print one copy of the worksheet, including the values obtained using the functional formulas.

MISCELLANEOUS

EXERCISE 54

Using Horizontal Table Lookup

- Enter the following information in columns A to G as shown below. (Option: Retrieve file <u>EXER54</u>.)

	A	B	C	D	E	F	G
1	Payroll Records						
2	==						
3	Employee Number:	300	301	302	303	304	305
4	Current Wage:	11.95	10.75	12.55	8.75	12.35	9.65
5	Previous Wage:	10.25	9.75	10.85	8.25	11.45	9.53
6	==						

- In the space below enter the functional formula needed in cell A8 to look up the current wage for employee 303.

  A8 _____

- Enter the formula in the worksheet.
- Enter the functional formula in cell A9 needed to look up the current wage for employee 301.
- Enter the functional formula in cell B8 needed to look up the previous wage for employee 303.
- Enter the functional formula in cell B9 needed to look up the previous wage for employee 301.
- Print one copy of the completed worksheet, including the values obtained while using the functional formulas.

EXERCISE 55 Using Manual Calculation

MISCELLANEOUS

- Enter the following information in columns A to D as shown below. (Option: Retrieve file EXER55.)
- Format all values, except for the ones in columns A and B, for 2 decimal places.

```
          A            B           C           D           E         F         G
 1   Payroll Record
 2   =============================================
 3      Employee     Hours       Wage        Gross
 4       Number      Worked      Rate         Pay
 5   ---------------------------------------------
 6        1001          36       8.60
 7        1002          40      10.50
 8        1003          40       9.50
 9        1004          38       6.80
10        1005          40       8.80
11   ---------------------------------------------
12        Total:                xxxxxxxxx
13      Average:
14      Highest:
15   =============================================
```

- Which of the function keys is used to initiate calculation while in the manual calculation mode?

  _____

- Enter the menu commands needed to switch to manual calculation.
- Enter the formula in cell D6 that is needed to compute gross pay for the first employee (Hours Worked times Wage Rate). Then copy the formula into cells D7 to D10.
- Press the function key needed to initiate calculation. Notice that all formulas are computed at once in cells D7 to D10.
- Enter appropriate formulas in cells B12 to B14. Then copy the formulas, as appropriate, into the blank cells on rows 12 to 14.
- Press the function key to initiate calculation.
- Format values appropriately.
- Save the file as EXER55.
- Print one copy of the worksheet.

EXERCISE 56   Making an ASCII File

- Retrieve file <u>EXER55</u>, created in Exercise 55. The worksheet should appear as shown below.

```
              A            B          C          D          E          F          G
 1   Payroll Record
 2   ==============================================
 3         Employee      Hours       Wage      Gross
 4          Number      Worked       Rate        Pay
 5   ----------------------------------------------
 6           1001          36        8.60     309.60
 7           1002          40       10.50     420.00
 8           1003          40        9.50     380.00
 9           1004          38        6.80     258.40
10           1005          40        8.80     352.00
11   ----------------------------------------------
12          Total:        194  xxxxxxxxx     1720.00
13        Average:       38.8        8.84      344.00
14        Highest:         40       10.50      420.00
15   ==============================================
```

- Save the worksheet as an ASCII file using the following file name: <u>EXER56</u>
- List the worksheet files on your screen. Notice that the above file name does not appear since it was not saved as a worksheet file.
- List the print files on your screen. Notice that the above file name appears on your screen. Also, notice the file extension.
- What three letters are used for the ASCII file extension above? _____

MISCELLANEOUS

EXERCISE 57

Integrated Reinforcement

- Enter the following information in columns A to G as shown below. Notice that column D of the vertical table is blank. Note: Values for this exercise are not stored on the disk and should be entered by the user exactly as shown below.

	A	B	C	D	E	F	G
1	Local Delivery Rate Charges				Weight	Category	Charges
2	=================================				=============================		
3	Weight	Category	Category		6	One	
4	(Ounces)	One	Two		4	One	
5	---------------------------------				12	Two	
6	1	0.32	0.32		13	One	
7	2	0.49	0.49		7	Two	
8	3	0.66	0.66		2	Two	
9	4	0.84	0.79		10	Two	
10	5	1.00	0.91		8	One	
11	6	1.17	1.00		8	Two	
12	7	1.34	1.11		5	Two	
13	8	1.51	1.32		=============================		
14	9	1.68	1.45				
15	10	1.85	1.40				
16	11	2.02	1.50				
17	12	2.19	1.55				
18	13	2.59	1.85				
19	14	2.69	1.93				
20	=================================						

- You will use the @VLOOKUP function to compute the charges in column G. In the space below write the functional formula needed to determine the first charge.

  G3 _____

- Enter the formula in the worksheet. Enter the remaining formulas in cells G4 to G12 to look up the other prices.
- Print one copy of the worksheet, including column G.
- Freeze the horizontal titles on the screen. Move the cell pointer to cell A35. Note that the titles remain on the screen. Unfreeze the titles.
- Save the file with the following file name: EXER57
- List the files on the screen. Notice that file EXER57 is on the list.
- Delete the following file from the disk: EXER57
- List the files on the screen. Notice that file EXER57 is no longer on the screen since it was deleted from the disk prior to listing files on the screen.

EXERCISE 58 Using Single Variable Values

DECISION MAKING

- Enter the following information in columns A to F as shown below. (Option: Retrieve file UNDERLINE_EXER58.) Note: If you are not using the data disk to retrieve files, save this partially completed worksheet as EXER59. It will be used as a part of Exercise 59.

```
            A              B          C         D         E           F            G
 1   Medical Statement - Overdue Accounts
 2   ==============================================================
 3                                           Days    5 Days    Over 5 Days
 4          Name         Service     Amount  Overdue  Overdue     Overdue
 5   --------------------------------------------------------------
 6   Chin, J.     Exam            65        3
 7   Cruz, D.     Stitches        45        5
 8   Duffy, R.    X-Rays          75        8
 9   Everex, C.   Exam            65       10
10   Hite, W.     Tests           78        5
11   Perez, R.    Exam            65       18
12   ==============================================================
```

- In the space below write the logical formula needed to place a 1 in cell E6 if the days overdue (cell D6) is exactly 5. Otherwise, a 0 should appear in the cell.

  E6 _____

- Enter the formula in the worksheet. Then copy the formula to the remaining cells in the column.
- Enter the formula in cell F6 needed to place a 1 in the cell if the days overdue is greater than 5. Otherwise, a 0 should appear in the cell. Then copy the formula to the remaining cells in the column.
- Print one copy of the worksheet.

EXERCISE 59 Using Logical Operators

- Enter the following information in columns A to E as shown below. (Option: Retrieve file <u>EXER59</u>.)

```
        A              B            C         D         E          F          G
1   Medical Statement - Overdue Accounts
2   ==================================================
3                                         Days      New
4       Name         Service      Amount  Overdue   Amount
5   -----------------------------------------------
6   Chin, J.      Exam            65         3
7   Cruz, D.      Stitches        45         5
8   Duffy, R.     X-Rays          75         8
9   Everex, C.    Exam            65        10
10  Hite, W.      Tests           78         5
11  Perez, R.     Exam            65        18
12  ==================================================
```

- In the space below write the formula (using @IF and logical operators) needed in cell E6 to add $5 to the amount if it is 5 or fewer days overdue. Otherwise, add $10 to the amount.

  E6 _____

- Enter the formula in the worksheet. Then copy the formula to the remaining cells in column E.
- Format all values, except column D, for 2 decimal places.
- Print one copy of the worksheet.

EXERCISE 60 — Using Logical Operators With Math

- Enter the following information in columns A to F as shown below. (Option: Retrieve file EXER60.)

```
       A            B          C        D          E          F         G
1  Sales Invoice
2  ===============================================================
3  Item                      List                Net        Total
4  ID          Quantity     Price Discount      Price       Cost
5  ---------------------------------------------------------------
6  P234             27      13.45
7  T284             13      13.65
8  T296             17      14.29
9  T297             39       5.98
10 W325             28      10.45
11 W345             32      18.97
12 W578             29      28.95
13 X782             28      36.73
14 X987             33      97.39
15 ---------------------------------------------------------------
16 Total
17 ===============================================================
```

- In the space below write the formula (using @IF and logical operators) needed in cell D6 to compute the discount based on the following: Reduce the list price by 25 percent if the quantity is over 30. Otherwise, reduce the list price by 10 percent.

  D6 _____

- Enter the formula in the worksheet. Then copy the formula to the remaining cells in column D. Add formulas needed to compute the total amounts.
- Enter and copy formulas in columns E and F.
- Note: Net price equals the list price minus the calculated discount. Total cost equals the net price amount times the quantity.
- Format all values, except column B, for 2 decimal places.
- Print one copy of the worksheet.

EXERCISE 61

Using a Logical Connective: OR

- Enter the following information in columns A to E as shown below. (Option: Retrieve file EXER61.)

```
         A              B         C       D          E          F
1   Employee Profile
2   ============================================================
3                  Years of                      Retirement
4        Name       Service      Age    Salary   Eligibility
5   ------------------------------------------------------------
6   Cortez, M.         32         53    34,000
7   Howvitz, P.        13         57    35,700
8   Jensen, M.          7         26    24,500
9   Keller, M.         34         53    37,250
10  Love, G.           26         43    31,680
11  Markus, F.         12         31    29,750
12  Perez, K.           3         22    28,450
13  ------------------------------------------------------------
14  Total Persons Eligible for Retirement:
15  ============================================================
```

- In the space below enter the logical operator (OR) and functional formula needed to place a 1 in cell E6 if Cortez, M. is eligible for retirement: at least 30 years of service "or" at least 55 years of age. Otherwise, a 0 should appear in the cell.

  E6 _____

- Enter the formula in the worksheet. Then copy the formula to the remaining cells in the column.
- Enter a formula in cell E14 to compute the total number eligible for retirement.
- Print one copy of the worksheet.

EXERCISE 62   Using a Logical Connective: AND

- Enter the following information in columns A to D as shown below. (Option: Retrieve file EXER62.)

	A	B	C	D	E	F	G
1	Overdue Invoices						
2	====================================						
3	Invoice	Days	Invoice				
4	No.	Overdue	Amount	Exception			
5	----------------------------------						
6	1001	12	1,200				
7	1002	13	1,300				
8	1003	9	1,400				
9	1004	15	800				
10	1005	14	700				
11	1006	5	500				
12	1007	16	1,400				
13	1008	15	800				
14	1009	14	1,200				
15	1010	16	600				
16	====================================						

- In the space below enter the logical operator (AND) and functional formula necessary to place the invoice number in cell D6 if the invoice is more than 10 days overdue "and" the amount is over $1,000. Otherwise, a 0 should appear in the cell.

  D6 _____

- Enter the formula in the worksheet. Then copy the formula to the remaining cells in the column.
- Print one copy of the worksheet.

EXERCISE 63

Integrated Reinforcement

- Enter the following information in columns A to F as shown below. Note: Values for this exercise are not stored on the disk.

	A	B	C	D	E	F	G
1	Payroll Register						
2	==						
3		Hours	Hourly	Regular	Overtime	Gross	
4	Name	Worked	Rate	Wages	Wages	Pay	
5	--						
6	Cortez, M.	40	7.5				
7	Howvitz, P.	44	8.5				
8	Jensen, M.	38	7.75				
9	Keller, M.	42	10.75				
10	Love, G.	44	9.5				
11	Markus, F.	40	12.85				
12	Miller, T.	32	9.75				
13	Perez, K.	40	12.5				
14	Rentzel, B.	46	8.95				
15	Kiser, B.	40	10.5				
16	Mertz, L.	44	12.5				
17	Oliphant, V.	42	9.75				
18	--						
19	Total						
20	==						

- Assume that employees earn one and one-half the hourly rate for all hours (Overtime Hours) worked in excess of 40 hours each week.
- In the spaces below write the functional formulas, using logical operators, to compute the values for cells D6, E6, and F6.

  D6 _____   E6 _____

  F6 _____

- Enter the formulas in the worksheet. Copy the formulas to the remaining cells in the columns. Then enter formulas needed to compute a total for each column.
- Format all values, except the ones in column B, for 2 decimal places.
- Print one copy of the worksheet.

EXERCISE 64 — Using a Range Format Macro

MACRO DEVELOPMENT

- Enter the following information in columns A to E as shown below. (Option: Retrieve file EXER64.) Note: If this worksheet was not retrieved from disk storage, save it prior to entering the macros with the following file name: EXER64

```
        A         B         C         D         E       F       G       H
1  Value Formats
2  ===================================================
3    345.235   345.235  1345.235     0.567   345.235
4      3.356     3.356     3.356     0.5432    3.356
5      5.326     5.326     5.326     0.0957    5.326
6     45.3      45.3      45.3       0.1075   45.3
7      3.231     3.231     3.231     0.0875    3.231
8      4.5534    4.5534    4.5534    0.0754    4.5534
9  ===================================================
```

- Enter a macro in cell A11 that will format column A for Currency Format with 2 decimal places.
- Enter a macro in cell A13 that will format column B for Fixed Format with 1 decimal place.
- Enter a macro in cell A15 that will format column C for Comma Format with 0 decimal places.
- Enter a macro in cell A17 that will format column D for Percent Format with 2 decimal places.
- Enter a macro in cell A19 that will format column E for Currency Format with 0 decimal places.
- Enter the name that will be assigned to the macro in the cell to the right of each macro—A for the first macro, B for the second macro, and so forth. Note: This is optional, but recommended.
- Enter a short description of each macro in the cell to the right of the name of each macro. Note: This is optional, but recommended.
- Use menu commands to name each macro.
- Invoke each macro individually. View the screen as you invoke each macro to determine format changes.
- Print one copy of the worksheet, including the macros.

EXERCISE 65   Using an Erase Worksheet Macro

- Enter the following information in columns A to E as shown below. (Option: Retrieve file <u>EXER64</u>.)

	A	B	C	D	E	F	G	H
1	Value Formats							
2	===							
3	345.235	345.235	1345.235	0.567	345.235			
4	3.356	3.356	3.356	0.5432	3.356			
5	5.326	5.326	5.326	0.0957	5.326			
6	45.3	45.3	45.3	0.1075	45.3			
7	3.231	3.231	3.231	0.0875	3.231			
8	4.5534	4.5534	4.5534	0.0754	4.5534			
9	===							

- Use the space below to indicate the coding necessary to write a macro to erase the entire worksheet from the screen.

  A11 _____

- Enter the macro in cell A11. Write the name of the macro in cell B11 (use E as the name in this instance). Write a description of the macro in cell C11.
- Name the macro.
- Save the worksheet using the following file name: <u>EXER65</u>
- Invoke the macro. Notice that the worksheet is erased from memory and the screen.
- Retrieve file <u>EXER65</u>. Note that the worksheet still resides on disk even though it has been erased from memory.
- Print one copy of the worksheet. Then invoke the macro a second time.

MACRO DEVELOPMENT

EXERCISE 66

Using a Print Macro

- Enter the following information in columns A to E as shown below. (Option: Retrieve file <u>EXER64</u>.)

```
        A         B         C          D         E        F        G        H
1  Value Formats
2  ================================================
3    345.235   345.235  1345.235     0.567   345.235
4      3.356     3.356     3.356     0.5432    3.356
5      5.326     5.326     5.326     0.0957    5.326
6       45.3      45.3      45.3     0.1075     45.3
7      3.231     3.231     3.231     0.0875    3.231
8     4.5534    4.5534    4.5534     0.0754   4.5534
9  ================================================
```

- Use the space below to indicate macro coding needed to print the worksheet.

  A11 _____

- Enter the macro in cell A11. Then write the macro name and description in cells C11 and D11.
- Name and invoke the macro. Note: Be sure your printer is ready before you invoke the macro.

EXERCISE 67   Using a Special Key
Macro

- Enter the following information in columns A to E as shown below. (Option: Retrieve file <u>EXER64</u>.)

```
          A         B         C         D         E       F       G       H
1    Value Formats
2    ==================================================
3     345.235   345.235 1345.235     0.567   345.235
4       3.356     3.356    3.356    0.5432     3.356
5       5.326     5.326    5.326    0.0957     5.326
6        45.3      45.3     45.3    0.1075      45.3
7       3.231     3.231    3.231    0.0875     3.231
8      4.5534    4.5534   4.5534    0.0754    4.5534
9    ==================================================
```

- Use the space below to indicate macro coding needed to move the cell pointer to the Home position.

    A11 _____

- Use the space below to indicate macro coding needed to make the cell pointer move to cell E6, change the value to 54.78, and then return to the Home position.

    A13 _____

- Enter the above macros in the worksheet. Then provide an appropriate name and description.
- Invoke each of the macros.
- Print one copy of the worksheet, including the macros.

MACRO DEVELOPMENT

EXERCISE 68

Using an Interactive Pause Macro

- Enter the following information in columns A to E as shown below. (Option: Retrieve file <u>EXER68</u>.) IMPORTANT: The entries on rows 5 to 13 will be entered as part of the exercise. Do <u>not</u> make entries on these rows until the macro is named and invoked.

```
          A                    B                    C         D       E
1  Address List
2  ========================================================================
3       Name          Street Address            City       State    ZIP
4  ------------------------------------------------------------------------
5  Beltz, Carl A.      112 W. Adams            Melbourne     FL     32202
6  Carson, Bill R.     6549 Lucas              Lima          OH     44843
7  Davis, Marilyn R.   6543 Ash                Atlanta       GA     30340
8  Ebbs, Rhonda T.     75 Morris St            Montclair     NJ     07860
9  Fultz, Randy E.     813 Botsford            Detroit       MI     48219
10 Getz, Mark W.       714 Acorn St            Chicago       IL     60620
11 Howard, Sara Y,.    11380 NW 27th Ave       Miami         FL     33167
12 Isley, Thomas W.    440 Davis St            San Francisco CA     94111
13 Perez, Juan K.      918 Ravena Rd           Boston        MA     02151
14
15 {?}{RIGHT}{?}{RIGHT}{?}{RIGHT}{?}{RIGHT}{?}{DOWN}{LEFT}
16 {LEFT}{LEFT}{LEFT}/XG\A~
```

- Notes: The macro on row 15 originates in cell A15. The continuation of the macro on row 16 originates in cell A16. This macro permits the user to make an entry and automatically move to the next entry—then return at the end of a row to begin the next row. You should review the commands in the macro.
- You should name the macro (use A as the name).
- Move to cell A5 and invoke the macro. Notice that you simply press <Return> after each entry to move to the cell for the next entry.
- Add a macro that will print the worksheet. Then invoke the macro to print one copy of the worksheet.

Name _____ Date _____ Section _____ Evaluation _____

EXERCISE 69
Using an Interactive Pause Macro

MACRO DEVELOPMENT

- Enter the following information in columns A and B as shown below. (Option: Retrieve file <u>EXER69</u>.) IMPORTANT: The entries on rows 5 to 12 will be entered as part of the exercise. Do <u>not</u> make entries on these rows until the macro is created, named, and invoked.

```
          A                B          C        D        E        F
 1  Test Scores
 2  ===================================
 3  Name              Score
 4  -----------------------------
 5  Blalock, Linda        85
 6  Boatwright, Joan      98
 7  Craig, Craig          76
 8  DeWitt, Bryant        87
 9  Gipson, Judith        95
10  Nagasawa, June        78
11  Salvagio, Carlton     83
12  Tercovich, Anne       67
13  -----------------------------
14  Average           83.625
15  ===================================
```

- Enter a macro in cells A17 and A18 that will permit you to make entries in cells A5 to A12 and B5 to B12 with a pause between each entry.
- Move the cell pointer to cell A5 prior to invoking the macro.
- Add 8 names and scores to the worksheet.
- Print one copy of the worksheet.

69

EXERCISE 70 Using Intelligent Macros

- Enter the following information in columns A and B as shown below. (Option: Retrieve file <u>EXER70</u>.)

```
        A         B          C        D        E        F        G        H
1   University Enrollment
2   ===================
3     Class     Number
4   -------------------
5   Freshman     5789
6   Sophomore    4632
7   Junior       3428
8   Senior       2119
9   Graduate      763
10  Other         342
11  -------------------
12  Total       17073
13  Average     2845.5
14  ===================
```

- Enter a macro in cell A15 that will pause to permit you to indicate the range to be formatted for Comma Format with 0 decimal places. Name the macro A.
- Enter a macro in cell A17 that will pause to permit you to indicate the range to be printed. Name the macro B.
- In columns C and D (to the right of the macros) indicate the name of each macro and a short description of each macro.
- Invoke macro A. Then invoke macro B.
- Print one copy of the worksheet, including the macros.

Name _____ Date _____ Section _____ Evaluation _____

EXERCISE 71   Using an Automatic Execution Macro

- Enter the following information in columns A and B as shown below. (Option: Retrieve file <u>EXER71</u>.)

```
        A         B        C      D      E      F      G      H
 1  University Enrollment
 2  ==================
 3    Class     Number
 4  ------------------
 5  Freshman    5,789
 6  Sophomore   4,632
 7  Junior      3,428
 8  Senior      2,119
 9  Graduate      763
10  Other         342
11  ------------------
12  Total      17,073
13  Average     2,846
14  ==================
```

- In the space below write an "automatic execute" macro that will automatically print the worksheet each time it is retrieved.

  A19 _____

- Enter the macro in cell A19. Name the macro 0. (Remember to precede the name with a \.)
- Save the worksheet as file <u>EXER71</u>.
- Retrieve the worksheet (EXER71). Notice that the worksheet should automatically print after it is retrieved.

MACRO DEVELOPMENT

EXERCISE 72   Developing a Master Macro File

MACRO DEVELOPMENT

- This exercise relates to "building" a master macro worksheet file. The macros can then be retrieved into other worksheets that are created. Use the space provided to write macros for the applications indicated. Then enter and name the macros. Note: Values for this exercise are not stored on disk.
- Develop a macro that will print a worksheet. Use a pause command for the print range.

  A3 _____

- Develop a macro that will format a range of cells for the Comma Format with 2 decimal places. Use a pause command for the range to be formatted.

  A5 _____

- Develop a macro that will go to cell D3, enter today's date (@TODAY), and format the date for the Year-Month-Day format.

  A7 _____

- Enter the three macros in the three cells indicated above. Also, provide the names in column D and brief descriptions beginning in column E, to the right of the macros. Name the macros A, B, and C respectively.
- Note: If macro C is executed, the column width will need to be widened to 10.
- Name the range A3 to E3 <u>PRINT</u>.
- Save the file using the following file name: <u>MACRO</u>
- Print a copy of the macros, including the names and descriptions.

EXERCISE 73 Using Master Macros

- Enter the following information in columns A to C as shown below. (Option: Retrieve file <u>EXER73</u>.)

```
            A              B          C         D        E        F        G
1   Monthly Budget
2   ======================================
3        Item        Expense    Income
4   ------------------------------------
5   Salary                         2250
6   Interest                        359
7   Rent             660
8   Car Note         339
9   Food             425
10  Clothing         125
11  Entertainment    135
12  Savings          250
13  Other            675
14  ------------------------------------
15  Total           2609        2609
16  ======================================
```

- Retrieve the print macro from the master macro file (created in Exercise 72) so that it appears in cell A19, the name appears in cell D19, and the description begins in cell E19.
- Rename the macro, since the macro name does not transfer with the macro.
- Invoke the retrieved print macro.

EXERCISE 74 Integrated Reinforcement

MACRO DEVELOPMENT

- Use the space below to write macros for the indicated applications. Note: Values for this exercise are not stored on disk.
- A macro to erase the entire worksheet:

  _____

- A macro to erase only cell B14:

  _____

- A macro to format a specified range (pause) for Currency Format with 2 decimal places:

  _____

- A macro that will move the cell pointer to cell B16 automatically each time the file is retrieved:

  _____

- Note: A worksheet will not be printed for this exercise.

EXERCISE 75 Constructing a Database

- Enter the following information in columns A to G as shown below. (Option: Retrieve file EXER75.)

```
        A           B          C        D    E      F       G        H        I
1                 SELECTED STUDENT DATABASE
2
3   ENG401                              Advanced Placement
4
5   =====================================================
6   ID No.   Last Name   First    MI  Grade Section  GPA
7   =====================================================
8
9       642798 Ashford    Miko     K    12      1    3.64
10      469836 Taylor     Lakecia  A    12      8    2.58
11      691805 Strickland Clay     R    12      8    4.00
12      573811 Combs      Brent    S    11      3    3.52
13      497203 Spann      Tamala   J    10      7    3.46
14      300567 Loflin     Lamar    N    11      5    2.16
15      721836 Loflin     Leigh    S    12      5    2.00
16      649714 Rowland    Carisa   D    11      7    3.28
17      443829 Loggins    Brian    K    12      6    4.00
18      642789 Nguyen     Ducphong S    10      5    4.56
19
20  =====================================================
```

- Format the values in column G for Fixed Format with 2 decimal places.
- Print one copy of the worksheet.
- Save the worksheet as EXER75.

EXERCISE 76 Sorting Numerically

- Retrieve file <u>EXER75</u>, saved in the previous exercise.
- The worksheet should appear as shown below.

```
          A          B          C       D     E        F        G        H         I
 1                 SELECTED STUDENT DATABASE
 2
 3   ENG401                                 Advanced Placement
 4
 5   ==================================================================
 6   ID No.   Last Name   First    MI Grade Section GPA
 7   ==================================================================
 8
 9      642798 Ashford    Miko     K     12       1   3.64
10      469836 Taylor     Lakecia  A     12       8   2.58
11      691805 Strickland Clay     R     12       8   4.00
12      573811 Combs      Brent    S     11       3   3.52
13      497203 Spann      Tamala   J     10       7   3.46
14      300567 Loflin     Lamar    N     11       5   2.16
15      721836 Loflin     Leigh    S     12       5   2.00
16      649714 Rowland    Carisa   D     11       7   3.28
17      443829 Loggins    Brian    K     12       6   4.00
18      642789 Nguyen     Ducphong S     10       5   4.56
19
20   ==================================================================
```

- Sort the spreadsheet numerically by ID No. using ascending sequence.
- Print one copy of the sorted worksheet.
- Sort the worksheet numerically by Grade and Section within each grade using ascending sequence.
- Print one copy of the sorted worksheet.

EXERCISE 77   Sorting Alphabetically

- Retrieve file <u>EXER75</u>, created in a previous exercise.
- The worksheet should appear as shown below.

```
        A          B          C        D    E      F       G        H        I
1                SELECTED STUDENT DATABASE
2
3   ENG401                                Advanced Placement
4
5   ==================================================================
6   ID No.   Last Name  First    MI  Grade Section GPA
7   ==================================================================
8
9      642798 Ashford    Miko      K      12       1    3.64
10     469836 Taylor     Lakecia   A      12       8    2.58
11     691805 Strickland Clay      R      12       8    4.00
12     573811 Combs      Brent     S      11       3    3.52
13     497203 Spann      Tamala    J      10       7    3.46
14     300567 Loflin     Lamar     N      11       5    2.16
15     721836 Loflin     Leigh     S      12       5    2.00
16     649714 Rowland    Carisa    D      11       7    3.28
17     443829 Loggins    Brian     K      12       6    4.00
18     642789 Nguyen     Ducphong  S      10       5    4.56
19
20  ==================================================================
```

- Sort the spreadsheet alphabetically by Last Name and First using ascending sequence.
- Print one copy of the sorted spreadsheet.
- Save the sorted spreadsheet as <u>EXER77</u>.

DATABASE MANAGEMENT

EXERCISE 78 Finding Records

- Retrieve file <u>EXER77</u>, created in a previous exercise.
- The worksheet should appear as shown below.

```
        A           B          C        D    E      F       G        H        I
1                   SELECTED STUDENT DATABASE
2
3   ENG401                                   Advanced Placement
4
5   =========================================================
6   ID No.   Last Name   First    MI  Grade Section GPA
7   =========================================================
8
9     642798 Ashford     Miko     K     12      1   3.64
10    573811 Combs       Brent    S     11      3   3.52
11    300567 Loflin      Lamar    N     11      5   2.16
12    721836 Loflin      Leigh    S     12      5   2.00
13    443829 Loggins     Brian    K     12      6   4.00
14    642789 Nguyen      Ducphong S     10      5   4.56
15    649714 Rowland     Carisa   D     11      7   3.28
16    497203 Spann       Tamala   J     10      7   3.46
17    691805 Strickland  Clay     R     12      8   4.00
18    469836 Taylor      Lakecia  A     12      8   2.58
19
20  =========================================================
```

- Create a criterion range in cells A25 to G25 for finding selected records.
- Search for and find all records for students with the last name Loflin.
- View the records on the screen as they are found.
- In the space provided below write the number of records found for students with the last name Loflin.

_____

- Search for and find all records for students in Grade 11.
- View the records on the screen as they are found.
- In the space provided below write the number of records found for students in Grade 11.

_____

- Save the workdsheet, including the criterion range, as <u>EXER78</u>.

EXERCISE 79

Finding Records Using Logical Relationships

- Retrieve file <u>EXER78</u>, created in a previous exercise.
- The worksheet should appear as shown below.

```
        A           B          C        D    E        F       G       H        I
1                SELECTED STUDENT DATABASE
2
3   ENG401                               Advanced Placement
4
5   =========================================================
6   ID No.   Last Name   First    MI  Grade Section GPA
7   =========================================================
8
9      642798 Ashford     Miko     K      12        1    3.64
10     573811 Combs       Brent    S      11        3    3.52
11     300567 Loflin      Lamar    N      11        5    2.16
12     721836 Loflin      Leigh    S      12        5    2.00
13     443829 Loggins     Brian    K      12        6    4.00
14     642789 Nguyen      Ducphong S      10        5    4.56
15     649714 Rowland     Carisa   D      11        7    3.28
16     497203 Spann       Tamala   J      10        7    3.46
17     691805 Strickland  Clay     R      12        8    4.00
18     469836 Taylor      Lakecia  A      12        8    2.58
19
20  =========================================================
```

- Search for and find all records for students with a GPA greater than 3.50.
- View the records on the screen as they are found.
- In the space provided below write the number of records found for students with a GPA greater than 3.50.

_____

- Search for and find all records for students with a GPA less than 3.00.
- View the records on the screen as they are found.
- In the space provided below write the number of records found for students with a GPA less than 3.00.

_____

DATABASE MANAGEMENT

EXERCISE 80 Extracting Records

- Retrieve file <u>EXER78</u>, created in a previous exercise.
- The worksheet should appear as shown below.

```
         A         B          C        D    E      F       G      H       I
 1                 SELECTED STUDENT DATABASE
 2
 3   ENG401                             Advanced Placement
 4
 5   =======================================================
 6   ID No.    Last Name  First    MI Grade Section GPA
 7   =======================================================
 8
 9     642798  Ashford    Miko     K     12      1   3.64
10     573811  Combs      Brent    S     11      3   3.52
11     300567  Loflin     Lamar    N     11      5   2.16
12     721836  Loflin     Leigh    S     12      5   2.00
13     443829  Loggins    Brian    K     12      6   4.00
14     642789  Nguyen     Ducphong S     10      5   4.56
15     649714  Rowland    Carisa   D     11      7   3.28
16     497203  Spann      Tamala   J     10      7   3.46
17     691805  Strickland Clay     R     12      8   4.00
18     469836  Taylor     Lakecia  A     12      8   2.58
19
20   =======================================================
```

- Create an extraction range in cells A30 to G30 for extracting selected records. Include all seven column headings at the top of the extraction range.
- Extract all records for students in Grade 10.
- Print one copy of the extracted records; include column headings.
- In the space provided below write the number of records extracted

  for Grade 10 students. _____
- Extract all records for students in Grade 11.
- Print one copy of the extracted records; include column headings.
- In the space provided below write the number of records extracted

  for Grade 11 students. _____
- Extract all records for students in Grade 12.
- Print one copy of the extracted records; include column headings.
- In the space provided below write the number of records extracted

  for Grade 12 students. _____
- Remove any extracted records from the extraction range prior to saving the worksheet.
- Save the worksheet as <u>EXER80</u>.

Name _____ Date _____ Section _____ Evaluation _____

EXERCISE 81 Using Multiple Criteria

- Retrieve file <u>EXER80</u>, created in a previous exercise.
- The worksheet should appear as shown below.

```
         A          B          C        D     E       F        G          H          I
1                  SELECTED STUDENT DATABASE
2
3     ENG401                                 Advanced Placement
4
5     ===============================================================
6     ID No.   Last Name   First    MI  Grade Section  GPA
7     ===============================================================
8
9      642798 Ashford     Miko      K      12       1    3.64
10     573811 Combs       Brent     S      11       3    3.52
11     300567 Loflin      Lamar     N      11       5    2.16
12     721836 Loflin      Leigh     S      12       5    2.00
13     443829 Loggins     Brian     K      12       6    4.00
14     642789 Nguyen      Ducphong  S      10       5    4.56
15     649714 Rowland     Carisa    D      11       7    3.28
16     497203 Spann       Tamala    J      10       7    3.46
17     691805 Strickland  Clay      R      12       8    4.00
18     469836 Taylor      Lakecia   A      12       8    2.58
19
20    ===============================================================
```

- Use multiple criteria to extract the records for all students in Section 8 of Grade 12.
- Print one copy of the extracted records, including column headings.
- In the space provided below write the number of records extracted for students in Section 8 of Grade 12.

_____

- Change the multiple criteria to extract the records for all Grade 12 students with a GPA of 4.00.
- Print one copy of the extracted records, including column headings.
- In the space provided below write the number of records extracted for Grade 12 students with a GPA of 4.00.

_____

DATABASE MANAGEMENT

81

EXERCISE 82 Eliminating Duplicate Records

- Enter the following information in columns A to D as shown below. (Option: Retrieve file <u>EXER82</u>.)

	A	B	C	D	E	F	G
1		HEALTHWRITE INSURANCE					
2		Policyholder Summary					
3							
4	==						
5		Policy	Last		Semiannual		
6		Number	Name	Age	Premium		
7		5038619	Coscia	28	$387.56		
8		4279118	Walters	52	$409.00		
9		3225065	Clifton	56	$374.55		
10		5038619	Coscia	28	$387.56		
11		4391226	Uhls	37	$582.10		
12		1480005	Workman	42	$436.80		
13		2569817	Carney	38	$410.00		
14		4297118	Whitehorn	24	$496.00		

- Create a criterion range for specifying the criteria for extraction.
- Create an extraction output range for displaying the extracted records.
- Extract all records for policyholders who are less than 30 years old using the "Unique" function.
- Records which are duplicated in the database should appear only once in the extraction output area.
- In the space provided below write the number of unique records extracted for policyholders who are less than 30 years old.

_____

- Delete any duplicate records from the original database.
- Print one copy of the extracted output range, including the heading information.

EXERCISE 83   Deleting Records

- Retrieve file <u>EXER80</u>, created in a previous exercise.
- The worksheet should appear as shown below.

```
        A           B          C        D   E      F       G        H         I
1                SELECTED STUDENT DATABASE
2
3   ENG401                              Advanced Placement
4
5   ==========================================================
6   ID No.    Last Name   First    MI Grade Section GPA
7   ==========================================================
8
9     642798  Ashford     Miko     K    12       1  3.64
10    573811  Combs       Brent    S    11       3  3.52
11    300567  Loflin      Lamar    N    11       5  2.16
12    721836  Loflin      Leigh    S    12       5  2.00
13    443829  Loggins     Brian    K    12       6  4.00
14    642789  Nguyen      Ducphong S    10       5  4.56
15    649714  Rowland     Carisa   D    11       7  3.28
16    497203  Spann       Tamala   J    10       7  3.46
17    691805  Strickland  Clay     R    12       8  4.00
18    469836  Taylor      Lakecia  A    12       8  2.58
19
20  ==========================================================
```

- Delete from the worksheet the records for all students in Grade 10.
- Print one copy of the remaining records after the selected records have been deleted.
- Delete from the remaining records the records for all students with a GPA less than 3.00.
- Print one copy of the worksheet after the selected records have been deleted.

Name _____ Date _____ Section _____ Evaluation _____

EXERCISE 84

Statistical Function @DSUM

- Enter the following information in columns A to H as shown below. (Option: Retrieve file <u>EXER84</u>.)

```
          A              B            C      D       E      F       G        H
1                              KENTWELL SOUP COMPANY
2                                  Sales Summary
3  ===================================================================================
4  Salesperson   Salesperson                   Quarters            Yearly
5  Number        Name          State First  Second Third  Fourth Total
6  ===================================================================================
7         4087  Benson         LA    82,600 76,201 79,402 84,552
8         4026  Barnhill       FL    48,550 54,172 52,806 55,374
9         5310  Hollingsworth  GA    61,380 60,358 60,481 62,840
10        8265  Shifflett      LA    92,368 88,560 86,505 92,658
11        5090  Guirlando      TX    74,162 75,482 76,385 77,203
12        8130  Saylor         FL    58,279 56,391 54,527 59,572
13        4096  Biggert        LA    60,481 62,587 63,889 64,666
14        4099  Bushnell       TX    38,274 40,351 40,254 41,811
15        5020  Cianciola      GA    76,508 72,964 73,916 77,482
16 ===================================================================================
17 TOTAL FOR STATE OF
```

- If needed, format all values in columns D to G for Comma Format with 0 decimal places.
- If needed, format the values in column H for Currency Format with 0 decimal places.
- In the space provided below write the formula to calculate the yearly total in cell H7.

  H7 _____

- Enter the formula in cell H7.
- Copy the formula into cell H7 to cells H8 to H15.
- Sort the worksheet alphabetically by State using ascending sequence.
- Save the sorted worksheet as <u>EXER84</u> prior to entering the following statistical functions.
- Create a criterion range in cells A20 to H20 to be used for selecting records to be included in the calculations.
- In the space provided below write the @DSUM statistical function to calculate total yearly sales for the state of Louisiana (LA).

  D17 _____

- Enter the statistical function in cell D17.
- Enter <u>LA</u> in cell C17.
- In the space provided below write the amount of total yearly sales for the state of Louisiana.

  _____

84 COPYRIGHT © 1990 BY McGRAW-HILL, INC. ALL RIGHTS RESERVED.

DATABASE MANAGEMENT

- The @DSUM statistical function to calculate total yearly sales for the state of Texas (TX) will be the same as the statistical function already entered in cell D17. Only the criteria should be changed from LA to TX.
- Enter TX in cell C17.
- In the space provided below write the amount of total yearly sales for the state of Texas.

———————————————

- Print one copy of the worksheet showing the total yearly sales for the state of Texas.

EXERCISE 85

Statistical Function @DAVG

DATABASE MANAGEMENT

- Retrieve file <u>EXER84</u>, created in a previous exercise.
- The worksheet should appear as shown below.

	A	B	C	D	E	F	G	H
1				KENTWELL SOUP COMPANY				
2				Sales Summary				
3	==							
4	Salesperson	Salesperson				Quarters		Yearly
5	Number	Name	State	First	Second	Third	Fourth	Total
6	==							
7	8130	Saylor	FL	58,279	56,391	54,527	59,572	$228,769
8	4026	Barnhill	FL	48,550	54,172	52,806	55,374	$210,902
9	5310	Hollingsworth	GA	61,380	60,358	60,481	62,840	$245,059
10	5020	Cianciola	GA	76,508	72,964	73,916	77,482	$300,870
11	4087	Benson	LA	82,600	76,201	79,402	84,552	$322,755
12	8265	Shifflett	LA	92,368	88,560	86,505	92,658	$360,091
13	4096	Biggert	LA	60,481	62,587	63,889	64,666	$251,623
14	5090	Guirlando	TX	74,162	75,482	76,385	77,203	$303,232
15	4099	Bushnell	TX	38,274	40,351	40,254	41,811	$160,690
16	==							
17	TOTAL FOR STATE OF							
18								

- Use the same criterion range previously created.
- Change the contents of cell A17 to AVERAGE FOR STATE OF instead of TOTAL FOR STATE OF.
- In the space provided below write the @DAVG statistical function to find the average yearly sales by salespeople from Florida (FL).

  D17 _____

- Enter the statistical function in cell D17.
- Enter <u>FL</u> in cell C17.
- In the space provided below write the average yearly sales for the state of Florida.

  _____

- The @DAVG statistical function to find the average yearly sales by salespeople from Georgia (GA) will be the same as that entered in cell D17 previously. Only the criteria should be changed from FL to <u>GA</u>.
- Enter GA in cell C17.
- In the space provided below write the average yearly sales for the state of Georgia.

  _____

- Print one copy of the worksheet showing the average yearly sales for the state of Georgia.

EXERCISE 86

Integrated Reinforcement

- Enter the following information in columns A to H as shown below. (Option: Retrieve file <u>EXER86</u>.)

	A	B	C	D	E	F	G
1			READER'S JOURNAL SUBSCRIPTIONS				
2			First Quarter				
3	**						
4	Subscriber			Address			
5	Last	First	Street	City	State	ZIP	Type
6	**						
7	Spivey	Lazandra	2056 Troutbeck Lane	Rochester	NY	14626	A
8	Yates	Mary	3288 Sinking Spring	Reading	PA	19608	S
9	Pruitt	Robert	808 Holiday Park	Pittsburgh	PA	15239	S
10	Gamble	Opal	551 Decastro Drive	Cheyenne	WY	82009	A
11	Culp	Shannon	202 Shaughnessy Lane	Eugene	OR	97401	A
12	Midha	Yatesh	128 Homecroft Road	Syracuse	NY	13206	S
13	Berger	Marion	1400 Jacobs Drive	York	PA	17407	A
14	Coburn	Erica	3998 Liberty Avenue	Spokane	WA	99207	A
15	Sudbury	Scott	4605 Natrona Place	Casper	WY	82601	S
16	**						
17	TOTAL ANNUAL SUBSCRIPTIONS						

	H	I	J	K	L	M	N	O
1								
2								
3	*********							
4								
5	Cost							
6	*********							
7	$32.95							
8	$18.95							
9	$18.95							
10	$32.95							
11	$32.95							
12	$18.95							
13	$32.95							
14	$32.95							
15	$18.95							
16	*********							

- Sort the worksheet numerically by ZIP Code, using descending sequence.
- Note: Be sure to include column H in the data range.
- Print one copy of the sorted worksheet.
- Sort the worksheet alphabetically by Last name, using ascending sequence.
- View the sorted worksheet on the screen.
- Sort the worksheet alphabetically by State and City within each state, using ascending sequence.

DATABASE MANAGEMENT

- Create a criterion range and an extraction range for selecting and extracting selected records.
- Extract all records for subscribers from Pennsylvania (PA).
- Print one copy of the extracted records, including column headings.
- Extract all records for Annual (A) subscribers.
- Print one copy of the extracted records, including column headings.
- Delete the record for Yates from the worksheet.
- In the space provided below write the @DSUM statistical function to calculate the total cost of Annual (A) subscriptions.

  D17 _____

- Enter the statistical function in cell D17.
- Print one copy of the worksheet.

EXERCISE 87

Entering Data for the Graph

- Enter the following information in columns A to D as shown below. (Option: Retrieve file EXER87.)

```
        A         B         C         D         E         F         G         H
1            CRESTMONT ELEMENTARY SCHOOL
2              Fall Enrollment Summary
3       @@@@@@@@@@@@@@@@@@@@@@@@@@@@@@@@@@@@@@@@
4       Grade       Males     Females    Total
5       @@@@@@@@@@@@@@@@@@@@@@@@@@@@@@@@@@@@@@@@
6       First        86        112
7       Second       74         98
8       Third        59         63
9       Fourth       82        106
1Ø      Fifth        65         76
11      Sixth        55         69
12      @@@@@@@@@@@@@@@@@@@@@@@@@@@@@@@@@@@@@@@@
13      TOTALS
```

- In the space provided below write the formula to calculate the total number of students enrolled in the first grade.

  D6 _____

- Enter the formula in cell D6.
- Copy the formula in cell D6 into cells D7 to D11.
- In the space provided below write the formula to calculate the total number of males enrolled in the school.

  B13 _____

- Enter the formula in cell B13.
- Copy the formula in cell B13 into cells C13 and D13.
- Print one copy of the worksheet.
- Save the worksheet as EXER87.

EXERCISE 88   Constructing a Pie Chart

- Retrieve file <u>EXER87</u>, created in a previous exercise.
- The worksheet should appear as shown below.

```
        A          B          C          D          E       F       G       H
1       CRESTMONT ELEMENTARY SCHOOL
2          Fall Enrollment Summary
3       @@@@@@@@@@@@@@@@@@@@@@@@@@@@@@@@@@@@@@@@
4       Grade      Males    Females     Total
5       @@@@@@@@@@@@@@@@@@@@@@@@@@@@@@@@@@@@@@@@
6       First         86        112       198
7       Second        74         98       172
8       Third         59         63       122
9       Fourth        82        106       188
10      Fifth         65         76       141
11      Sixth         55         69       124
12      @@@@@@@@@@@@@@@@@@@@@@@@@@@@@@@@@@@@@@@@
13      TOTALS       421        524       945
```

- Create a pie chart showing the total males and total females enrolled in the school as shown below.

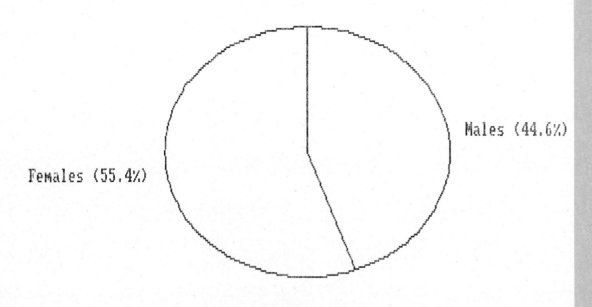

(Continued on Next Page)

- Use CRESTMONT ELEMENTARY SCHOOL as the first title and Fall Enrollment Summary as the second title to appear at the top of the pie chart.
- Use appropriate labels for each segment of the pie chart.
- View the pie chart on the screen.
- Save the pie chart as PIE88A.
- Print one copy of the pie chart.
- Create a second pie chart showing the total enrollments for each grade (first through sixth) as shown below.

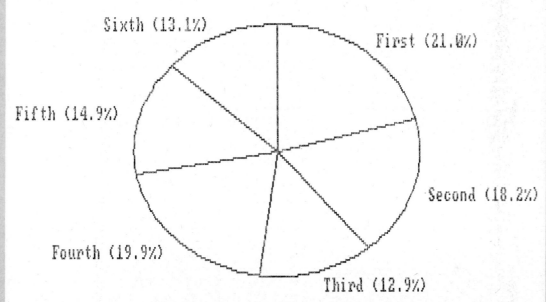

CRESTMONT ELEMENTARY SCHOOL
Fall Enrollment Summary

- Use appropriate first and second titles and labels for the pie chart.
- View the pie chart on the screen.
- Save the pie chart as PIE88B.
- Print one copy of the second pie chart.

EXERCISE 89 Constructing a Bar Graph

GRAPHING

- Retrieve file <u>EXER87</u>, created in a previous exercise.
- The worksheet should appear as shown below.

	A	B	C	D	E	F	G	H
1	CRESTMONT ELEMENTARY SCHOOL							
2	Fall Enrollment Summary							
3	@@							
4	Grade	Males	Females	Total				
5	@@							
6	First	86	112	198				
7	Second	74	98	172				
8	Third	59	63	122				
9	Fourth	82	106	188				
10	Fifth	65	76	141				
11	Sixth	55	69	124				
12	@@							
13	TOTALS	421	524	945				

- Create a bar graph showing the total enrollments for grades 1 through 6 as shown below.

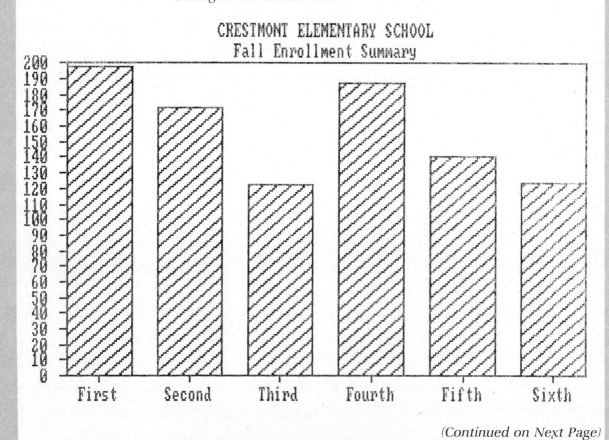

(Continued on Next Page)

- Use appropriate first and second titles and labels for the bar graph.
- View the bar graph on the screen.
- Save the bar graph as <u>BAR89A</u>.
- Print one copy of the bar graph.
- Revise the bar graph to show only the female enrollment for grades 1 through 6 as shown below.

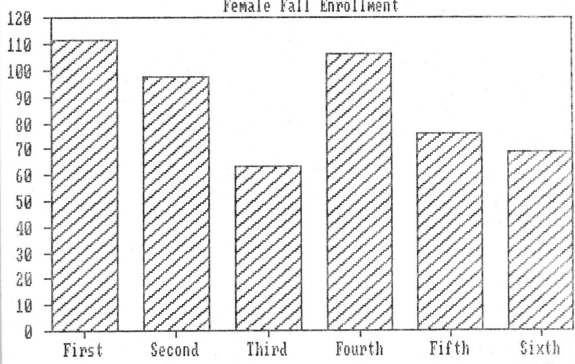

- Use appropriate first and second titles and labels for the bar graph.
- View the revised bar graph on the screen.
- Save the bar graph as <u>BAR89B</u>.
- Print one copy of the bar graph.

EXERCISE 90 Constructing a Multiple Bar Graph

- Retrieve file <u>EXER87</u>, created in a previous exercise.
- The worksheet should appear as shown below.

```
          A           B          C          D          E          F          G          H
1         CRESTMONT ELEMENTARY SCHOOL
2             Fall Enrollment Summary
3         @@@@@@@@@@@@@@@@@@@@@@@@@@@@@@@@@@@@@@@@@@@
4         Grade       Males      Females    Total
5         @@@@@@@@@@@@@@@@@@@@@@@@@@@@@@@@@@@@@@@@@@@
6         First          86         112        198
7         Second         74          98        172
8         Third          59          63        122
9         Fourth         82         106        188
10        Fifth          65          76        141
11        Sixth          55          69        124
12        @@@@@@@@@@@@@@@@@@@@@@@@@@@@@@@@@@@@@@@@@@@
13        TOTALS        421         524        945
```

- Create a multiple bar graph showing both the male and female enrollments for grades 1 through 6 as shown below.

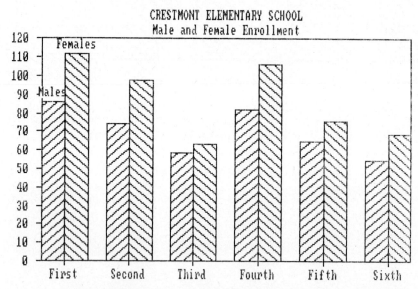

- Use appropriate first and second titles and labels for the multiple bar graph.
- View the multiple bar graph on the screen.
- Save the multiple bar graph as <u>BAR90</u>.
- Print one copy of the multiple bar graph.
- Save the worksheet as <u>EXER90</u>.

EXERCISE 91 Using Legends

- Retrieve file <u>EXER90</u>, created in a previous exercise.
- The worksheet should appear as shown below.

```
        A           B           C           D           E       F       G           H
1           CRESTMONT ELEMENTARY SCHOOL
2               Fall Enrollment Summary
3       @@@@@@@@@@@@@@@@@@@@@@@@@@@@@@@@@@@@@@
4       Grade       Males       Females     Total
5       @@@@@@@@@@@@@@@@@@@@@@@@@@@@@@@@@@@@@@
6       First          86         112          198
7       Second         74          98          172
8       Third          59          63          122
9       Fourth         82         106          188
10      Fifth          65          76          141
11      Sixth          55          69          124
12      @@@@@@@@@@@@@@@@@@@@@@@@@@@@@@@@@@@@@@
13      TOTALS        421         524          945
```

- View the multiple bar graph previously created.
- Create legends for the multiple bar graph to distinguish the male bar pattern from the female bar pattern as shown below.

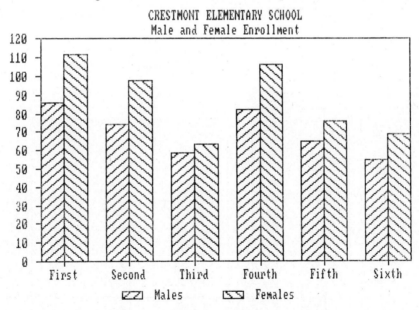

- View the revised bar graph on the screen.
- Save the multiple bar graph with legends as <u>BAR91</u>.
- Print one copy of the multiple bar graph with legends.
- Save the worksheet as <u>EXER91</u>.

EXERCISE 92 Using Axis Titles

- Retrieve file <u>EXER91</u>, created in a previous exercise.
- The worksheet should appear as shown below.

```
         A          B          C          D          E        F        G        H
1     CRESTMONT ELEMENTARY SCHOOL
2         Fall Enrollment Summary
3    @@@@@@@@@@@@@@@@@@@@@@@@@@@@@@@@@@@@@@@@
4    Grade       Males     Females     Total
5    @@@@@@@@@@@@@@@@@@@@@@@@@@@@@@@@@@@@@@@@
6    First          86        112        198
7    Second         74         98        172
8    Third          59         63        122
9    Fourth         82        106        188
10   Fifth          65         76        141
11   Sixth          55         69        124
12   @@@@@@@@@@@@@@@@@@@@@@@@@@@@@@@@@@@@@@@@
13   TOTALS        421        524        945
```

- View the multiple bar graph with legends previously created.
- Enter Grades 1-6 as an *x*-axis title to appear below the horizontal axis as shown below.
- Enter (Males and Females) as a *y*-axis title to appear to the left of the vertical axis as shown below.

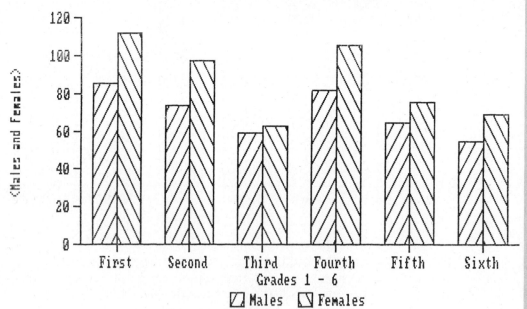

- Save the revised multiple bar graph as <u>BAR92</u>.
- Print one copy of the revised multiple bar graph with legends and axis titles.

EXERCISE 93   Changing the Scale

- Enter the following information in columns A to D as shown below. (Option: Retrieve file EXER93.)

```
        A              B            C          D       E        F         G
1              DOW JONES INDUSTRIAL AVERAGE
2                    Biggest Point Declines
3  ##########################################
4  Date           Points      Percentage
5  ##########################################
6  10-28-29        86.61         4.6%
7  01-08-86        61.87         3.3%
8  04-30-86        45.75         2.4%
9  06-09-86        41.91         2.3%
10 07-07-86        39.10         2.5%
11 09-11-86        38.33        12.8%
12 ##########################################
```

- Format the values in column B for Fixed Format with 2 decimal places.
- Format the values in column C for Percent Format with 1 decimal place.
- Create a bar graph showing the point declines in the Dow Jones Industrial Average from 10-28-29 to 09-11-86 as shown below.

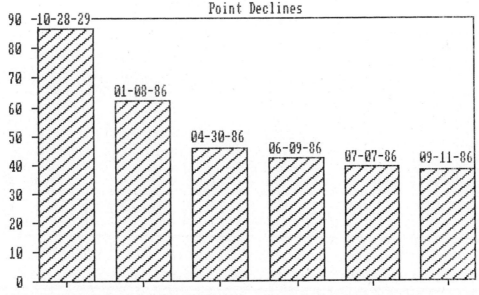

- Use appropriate first and second titles and labels.
- View the bar graph on the screen.
- Change the y-axis scale upper limit to 95.
- View the revised bar graph on the screen.
- Save the bar graph as BAR93.
- Print one copy of the revised bar graph.

EXERCISE 94

Constructing a Multiple Line Graph

- Retrieve file <u>EXER84</u>, created in a previous exercise.
- The worksheet should appear as shown below.

```
        A              B           C      D       E       F       G       H
1                           KENTWELL SOUP COMPANY
2                                Sales Summary
3  ===============================================================================
4  Salesperson    Salesperson                  Quarters            Yearly
5  Number         Name        State First  Second Third   Fourth  Total
6  ===============================================================================
7        8130     Saylor        FL    58,279 56,391 54,527 59,572 $228,769
8        4026     Barnhill      FL    48,550 54,172 52,806 55,374 $210,902
9        5310     Hollingsworth GA    61,380 60,358 60,481 62,840 $245,059
10       5020     Cianciola     GA    76,508 72,964 73,916 77,482 $300,870
11       4087     Benson        LA    82,600 76,201 79,402 84,552 $322,755
12       8265     Shifflett     LA    92,368 88,560 86,505 92,658 $360,091
13       4096     Biggert       LA    60,481 62,587 63,889 64,666 $251,623
14       5090     Guirlando     TX    74,162 75,482 76,385 77,203 $303,232
15       4099     Bushnell      TX    38,274 40,351 40,254 41,811 $160,690
16 ===============================================================================
17 TOTAL FOR STATE OF
```

- Sort the worksheet numerically by Salesperson Number using ascending sequence.
- Create a line graph showing the sales amounts for Quarters 1 and 2 (columns D and E) as shown below.

(Continued on Next Page)

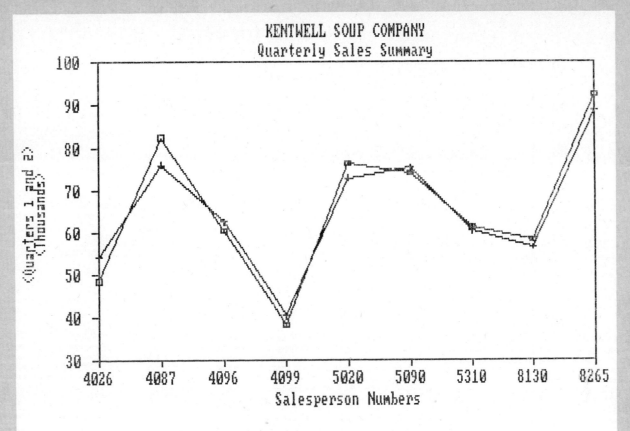

- Use appropriate first and second titles and axis titles.
- View the multiple line graph on the screen.
- Save the line graph as <u>LINE94A</u>.
- Print one copy of the line graph.
- Create a second line graph showing the sales for Quarters 1, 2, 3, and 4 (columns D, E, F, and G) as shown below.

(Continued on Next Page)

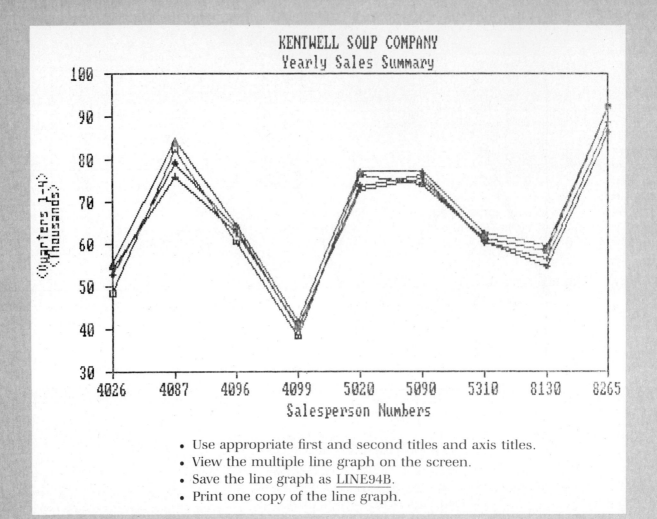

- Use appropriate first and second titles and axis titles.
- View the multiple line graph on the screen.
- Save the line graph as LINE94B.
- Print one copy of the line graph.

EXERCISE 95

Constructing an XY Graph

- Enter the following information in columns A to C as shown below. (Option: Retrieve file EXER95.)

	A	B	C	D	E	F	G
1	HIGHWAY'S USED CAR SALES						
2	Weekly Revenue Summary						
3							
4	Region	Cars Sold	Revenue				
5							
6	N	32	$12,160				
7	S	29	$8,700				
8	E	16	$6,080				
9	W	50	$22,500				
10							

- Format the values in column C for Currency Format with 0 decimal places.
- Create an XY graph showing the cars sold on the horizontal (x) axis and the revenue from car sales on the vertical (y) axis as shown below.

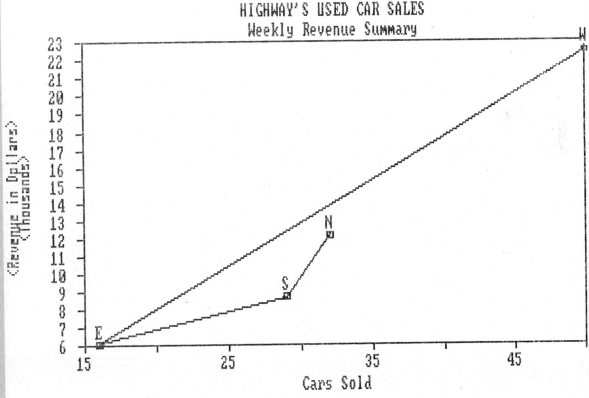

- Use appropriate titles and labels.
- View the XY graph on the screen.
- Save the XY graph as XY95.
- Print one copy of the XY graph.

101

EXERCISE 96 Integrated Reinforcement

GRAPHING

- Enter the following information in columns A to C as shown below. (Option: Retrieve file EXER96.)

	A	B	C	D	E	F
1		DISEASE PREVENTION				
2	United States and Developing Nations					
3						
4	**					
5	Disease	Cases Per Year	Deaths			
6	**					
7						
8	Influenza	19,000,000	28,000			
9	Pneumonia	8,500,000	7,500			
10	Meningitis	6,518,000	600,800			
11	Malaria	200,000,000	2,000,000			
12	Typhoid Fever	16,000,000	500,000			
13						
14	**					
15	TOTALS					
16	**					

- Format all values for Comma Format with 0 decimal places.
- In the space provided below write the formula to calculate total cases per year.

  B15 _____

- Enter the formula in cell B15.
- Copy the formula in cell B15 into cell C15.
- Use appropriate titles, labels, and legends for each graph.
- Create a pie chart showing the five diseases and the number of cases per year as shown below.

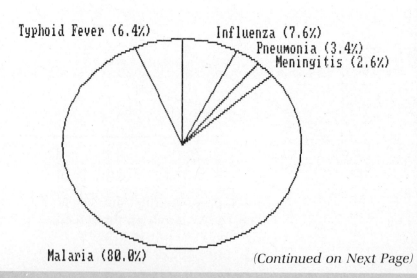

DISEASE PREVENTION
United States and Developing Nations

Typhoid Fever (6.4%)   Influenza (7.6%)
Pneumonia (3.4%)
Meningitis (2.6%)

Malaria (80.0%)

(Continued on Next Page)

- View the pie chart on the screen.
- Save the pie chart as <u>PIE96A</u>.
- Print one copy of the pie chart.
- Revise the pie chart to show only deaths caused by typhoid fever, meningitis, and malaria in a year as shown below.

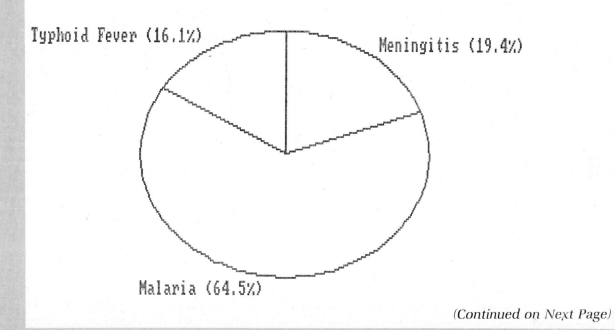

DISEASE PREVENTION
Resulting Deaths Per Year

Typhoid Fever (16.1%)

Meningitis (19.4%)

Malaria (64.5%)

(Continued on Next Page)

- View the revised pie chart on the screen.
- Save the pie chart as <u>PIE96B</u> and print one copy of the revised pie chart.
- Create a bar graph showing the cases per year for the five diseases as shown below.

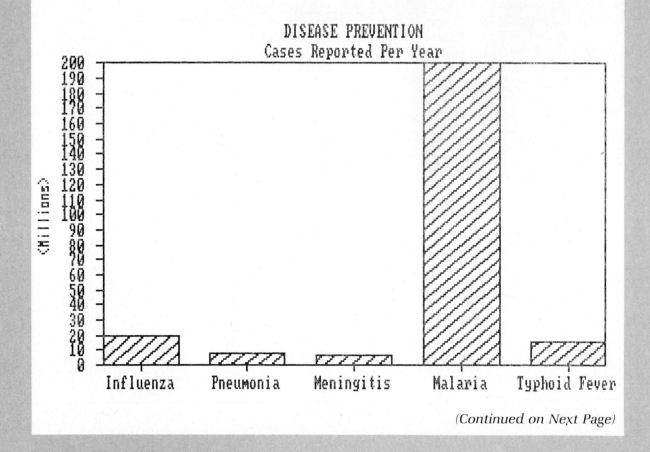

(Continued on Next Page)

- View the bar graph on the screen.
- Save the bar graph as <u>BAR96A</u> and print one copy of the bar graph.
- Create a line graph showing the cases per year for each of the five diseases as shown below.

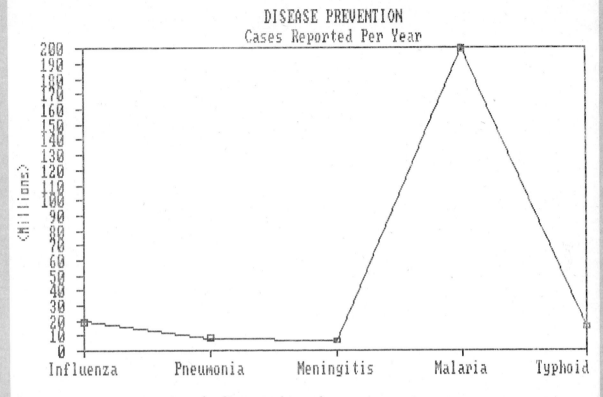

- View the line graph on the screen.
- Save the line graph as <u>LINE96A</u> and print one copy of the graph.

EXERCISE 97   Payroll Register

• Enter the following information in columns A to F as shown below. Note: Values for the exercise are not stored on disk.

```
        A          B          C         D          E          F          G          H
 1  Payroll Register
 2  =========================================================================
 3  Employee    Hours         Pay  Overtime   Regular    Gross
 4       ID    Worked        Rate       Pay       Pay      Pay
 5  -----------------------------------------------------------------
 6      1023       40        6.20
 7      1024       38        7.40
 8      1025       42        7.50
 9      1026       40        6.40
10      1027       44        6.40
11      1028       40        6.40
12      1029       40        8.60
13      1030       34        7.75
14      1031       36        8.80
15      1032       40        8.85
16      1033       36        7.75
17      1034       34        8.80
18      1035       40        9.60
19      1036       42       10.25
20      1037       42        9.50
```

• Use the @IF functional formula to compute overtime pay and regular pay based on the assumption that overtime pay is equal to one and one-half times the pay rate for all hours worked in excess of 40 hours each week. Format values in columns D to F for Fixed Format with 2 decimal places.
• Set horizontal titles after row 5. Then add payroll information for the following employees in columns A to C beginning on row 21:

```
1038        42        6.80
1039        38        8.50
1040        46       10.85
1041        36        8.80
```

• Copy formulas necessary to complete columns D to F for the additional employees.
• Print one copy of the worksheet.

EXERCISE 98 Inventory Record

- Enter the following information in columns A to D as shown below. Note: Values for this exercise are not stored on disk.

```
           A             B            C        D        E       F       G
1  Inventory Record
2  ============================================
3  Beginning Balance:                         450
4  --------------------------------------------------
5  Date            Purchased      Sold   Balance
6  --------------------------------------------------
7  1/23                  45
8  2/12                                  35
9  2/26                                 120
10 3/15                 200
11 4/21                  50
12 4/23                                 250
13 5/16                                  20
14 6/12                 100
15 6/22                                  60
16 7/14                                 125
17 8/25                 180
18 9/30                                  85
19 10/22                                110
20 11/8                  85
```

- Use the space below to write the formula needed to compute the balance after the 1/23 transaction.

  D7 _____

- Use the space below to write the formula needed to compute the balance after the 2/12 transaction.

  D8 _____

- Enter the formulas in the worksheet. Then copy the formula from cell D8 into cells D9 to D20.
- Print one copy of the worksheet.

107

EXERCISE 99   Mortgage Payment Schedule

- Enter the following information in columns A to E as shown below. Note: Values for this exercise are not stored on disk.

```
        A          B          C            D            E         F
 1  Mortgage Payment Schedule
 2  ========================================================
 3  Mortgage Loan Amount:                             185,000
 4  Years in Payment Period:                               30
 5  Annual Interest Rate:                              10.5%
 6  --------------------------------------------------------
 7  Monthly Payment:
 8  ========================================================
 9     Month                  Interest      Principal      Loan
10    Number      Payment     Applied        Applied      Balance
11  --------------------------------------------------------
```

- Number the months consecutively in column A.
- Use the space below to write the functional formula needed to compute the monthly payment needed to retire the loan.

    E7 _____

- Enter the formulas needed to compute the payment amount, interest amount applied, principal amount applied, and loan balance for the first month (cells B12 to E12).
- Enter the formulas needed to compute the payment amount, interest amount applied, principal amount applied, and loan balance for the second month (cells B13 to E13).
- Copy the formulas from B13 to E13 into the remainder of the worksheet.
- Print one copy of the worksheet.
- Expand the number of months from 9 to 36. Copy formulas needed to expand the worksheet.
- Print one copy of the worksheet.
- Change the loan amount to 120,000 in cell E3.
- Notice that the entire schedule is recalculated.
- Move the cell pointer to cell E3. Change the loan amount to 12,000.
- Move the cell pointer to E4. Change the payment period to 3 years.
- Assume that this is a loan for an automobile. What is the loan balance at the end of the first year? _____
- Change the figures in cells E3 to E5 to correspond with purchases that you may be considering—an automobile, furniture, new house, jewelry, and so forth. You may want to save this file as EXER99 for use when making future purchase considerations.

EXERCISE 100
Accounting Income Statement

- Enter the following information in columns A to D as shown below. Note: This file is not stored on disk.

```
              A                          B         C          D
 1  Income Statement                                       Percent
 2  ================================================of Sales
 3  Revenue:                                               ---------
 4    Sales                                      45,000
 5
 6  Cost of Goods Sold                           11,700
 7
 8  Gross Profit on Sales
 9
10  Operating Expenses:
11    Salaries Expense              12,450
12    Delivery Expense               6,500
13    Supplies Expense               2,950
14    Utilities Expense              1,670
15    Miscellaneous Expenses           250
16       Total Operating Expenses
17
18  Net Income
19  ==============================================================---------
```

- Enter the needed formula in cell C8 to compute gross profit on sales.
- Enter the needed formula in cell C16 to compute total operating expenses.
- Enter the needed formula in cell C18 to compute net income.
- Enter the formulas in column D needed to compute the percent that each other value in the income statement is related to sales revenue.
- Format values in columns B and C for Comma Format with 0 decimal places. Format values in column D for Percent Format with 2 decimal places.
- Print one copy of the worksheet.

EXERCISE 101

Personal Budget

- Enter the following information in columns A to E as shown below. Note that column D is blank in this example. Note: Values for this exercise are not stored on disk.

```
         A                    B          C         D       E        F       G
1   Personal Budget
2   ==========================================
3                                      Percent      Income
4          Item            Amount    of Income    Available
5   ------------------------------------------    **********
6   Rent                     725                    $2,800
7   Utilities                198                   **********
8   Car payment              235
9   Car expenses              85
10  Clothing.                 75
11  Food                     350
12  Medical                   97
13  Entertainment            240
14  Insurance                225
15  Credit card              245
16  Savings
17  Miscellaneous            106
18  ----------------------------------------
19  Total Expenses
20  ==========================================
```

- Use the space below to write a formula that will compute the total of the expenditures and deduct this total from the income available (cell E6) so that funds left over will automatically be budgeted for savings.

  B16 _____

- Enter the formula in the worksheet.
- Enter a formula in cell B19 to compute total expenses. Compare this amount with income available to make sure that they are comparable.
- Enter a formula in cell C6 to compute the percent of income available represented by rent. Then copy this formula to the remainder of the column.
- Format the values in column D for Percent Format with 1 decimal place.
- Print one copy of the worksheet.
- Change the amount in cell E6 to 3200. Then print one copy of the revised worksheet.
- Revise the amounts on the worksheet to represent a typical budget for your personal income and expenditures.
- Print one copy of the worksheet containing a budget for your personal income and expenditures.

Tutorial for 101 Advanced Spreadsheet Exercises

Using Lotus 1-2-3, VP-Planner, and Twin.

This tutorial is designed to assist the learning process when used with *101 Advanced Spreadsheet Exercises*. The tutorial can be used with Lotus 1-2-3 and software clones such as VP-Planner and Twin. You will be given specific commands to use the first time that a new task is presented. Many of these same tasks will be incorporated into subsequent exercises. However, the commands needed to complete tasks presented with an earlier exercise will not generally be repeated. You can either execute the command because you have already learned it or you can refer to the exercise where the command was introduced. This procedure will make the learning of Lotus 1-2-3 commands easy and illustrate ways that this popular software program can be used in the shortest amount of time possible.

To use this tutorial, you will need a copy of the *101 Advanced Spreadsheet Exercises* textbook, spreadsheet software (such as Lotus 1-2-3 or VP-Planner), and the optional data disk. This optional data disk can be used to save keyboarding time, since a large portion of many exercises has already been stored on the disk. Ask your instructor about whether you will be using the data disk while completing the exercises. If you are using spreadsheet software other than Lotus 1-2-3 (or clones such as VP-Planner and Twin) and an IBM-PC microcomputer (or your instructor does not want you to use a data disk), you will need to enter all information shown in the exercise template rather than retrieving it from the data disk.

Instructions assume that the user has first accessed the worksheet software and has an empty worksheet available on the monitor prior to beginning each exercise. The cell pointer should be in the Home (A1) position to begin each exercise.

When entering commands shown in this tutorial, all underlined characters should be typed, such as type / File Save EXER22 then press <Return>. In this example, the user will actually type /FSEXER22 and press the <Return> key. Notice that the following symbols are used to indicate a key that should be pressed: <>.

Do not enter characters in the tutorial that are not underlined. For example, assume that the following command sequence was given. Format column D for the Fixed Format with 2 decimal places by entering the following commands: / Range Format Fixed 2 <Return> D1.D10 <Return>. You should enter the following without the ending period: / RFF2 <Return> D1.D10 <Return>.

You should carefully read the specific instructions included with each exercise in the textbook. Study the menu selections on your monitor as you enter commands in order to become familiar with commands needed to perform various worksheet functions. Do not "just enter characters" that execute the commands. If you forget how to perform a function, refer to the earlier exercise instructions where the function was introduced or ask your instructor for assistance.

The instructions provided in this tutorial assume that you are using the data disk. Otherwise you will have to prepare the template as shown on the textbook prior to completing the instructions. The template contains only basic functions, so this should not

111

create a problem; however, extra time will be required to prepare the template. Regardless, this tutorial will serve as a valuable reference while completing exercises and later in a job-related environment.

If you are not using the data disk, you should provide appropriate column widths, value formats, label prefixes, rulings, and other functions so that your template appears like the one shown in the text.

IMPORTANT: If you are using the data disk, files have been stored into a directory named A101. If you are instructed in the text to retrieve file EXER14 and a data disk is in Drive B, you will enter / File Retrieve B: A101\EXER14 and press <Return>.

FILE DIRECTORY STRUCTURE

Root	Sub	File
B:\ $\longrightarrow$	A101\ $\longrightarrow$	EXER14.WKS

Entry:　　B:\A101\EXER14.WKS

By grouping original files in this directory on the data disk, you will be less likely to accidentally delete or modify them. Also, a maximum of 114 files can be stored on a 360K disk unless directories are used. A general procedure will be to retrieve a file from the data disk directory (as illustrated above), make revisions to the template, and then save the revised worksheet. To save a revised worksheet, enter / File Save B:EXER14 and press <Return> to save your final worksheet for Exercise 14 on the disk located in Drive B. With this procedure, the original file needed for the exercise is left unchanged in the directory (A101) and your revised file is stored on disk, but not in the directory A101. Of course, you will enter the appropriate drive designation that corresponds to the drive where your data disk is located, such as A: for Drive A, B: for Drive B, or C: for Drive C.

The text will instruct you to retrieve a specific file such as EXER1. Remember that

you must enter the drive designation (such as B:) and the directory (such as A101) prior to entering the file name for files stored in a directory. Spaces are not allowed. Note that a backslash (\) is used to separate the directory from the file name.

The worksheet file name extension, (WKS) for earlier versions of Lotus 1-2-3 or (WK1) for later versions of Lotus 1-2-3, does not need to be entered when retrieving or saving files. Files on the data disk have the WKS extension, but can be used with earlier or later versions of Lotus 1-2-3 (or spreadsheet software clones).

EXERCISE 1 - Entering Text and Values

- Notice that the data in column B have quotation marks (") as the label prefix to display the entries as right-aligned in the cells.
- View the monitor and answer the questions given in the text.
- Type / Worksheet Erase Yes to clear the file from your monitor and memory. Remember that the file still resides on the disk.

EXERCISE 2 - Using Label Prefixes and Saving a File

- The ∧ symbol is used as a prefix to a label entry to center the entry in the cell. The " symbol is used as a prefix to a label entry to right-align the entry in the cell. The ' is the default label prefix and is used to left-align the entry in the cell.
- Type / File Save EXER2 <Return> to save the worksheet onto the disk. Note: Since you probably do not want to save your file in the directory, you will enter only the drive designation (such as B:) before the file name—unless the desired drive is also the default drive.
- Type / Worksheet Erase Yes to erase the worksheet from the monitor and begin the next exercise. Note: You should execute these commands, to clear the memory and monitor, for each exercise prior to beginning the next exercise throughout the text.

EXERCISE 3 - Retrieving and Printing a Worksheet

- Since this file was saved as EXER2 during completion of Exercise 2 and is not in the directory, type / File Retrieve EXER2 and then press <Return>.
- Note: Unless the default drive is the same one containing the file, you should enter the drive designation in front of the file name, such as B:EXER2.
- To change the contents of a cell, move the cell pointer to the appropriate cell location, enter the desired characters, and then press <Return>.
- See Exercise 2 for instructions for saving the worksheet.
- Make sure your printer is ready to print. Then type / Print Printer Range A1.D16 and press <Return>. Type Align Go and the printer should begin. Type Page to move to the top of the next page. Type Quit to leave the Print menu. Note: These basic commands will be executed each time a worksheet is to be printed.

EXERCISE 4 - Using the Help Facility With Lotus 1-2-3

- Press <F1> to enter the Help facility.
- In addition to following instructions shown in the text, try other options. Then press <Esc> to exit the facility.

EXERCISE 5 - Formatting Values

- If you are using the optional data disk, type / File Retrieve A:\A101\EXER5 and then press <Return> to load the file from disk into memory and monitor display. Note that the drive designation (A: above) should be the actual name of the drive where the data disk is located. (If needed, review the above instructions that describe how to retrieve a file from a directory.) Otherwise, enter the information in the template prior to completing the exercise.
- Note: You will not be given the above instruction in the tutorial for subsequent ex-ercises, but the option will be mentioned in the text along with instructions for completion of the exercises.
- Move the cell pointer to cell A1. To change the values in column A to the Fixed Format with one place to the right of the decimal point, type / Range Format Fixed 1 <Return> A1.A15 <Return>. Note: Column A should now be changed to the desired format.
- Note: An alternative to typing the range (A1.A15 in this example) is to move the cell pointer to the end of the range (A15 in this example) and then press <Return>. Instructions throughout this tutorial will identify the affected range. However, you always have the option of using either the "typing" or the "pointing" method to identify the range. Try both methods to determine the one you prefer.
- To format the values in column B, move the pointer to cell B1. Then type / Range Format Percent 1 <Return> B1.B15 <Return>.
- The above steps will be used to format columns C to E for the desired formats.

EXERCISE 6 - Entering Formulas

- Move the cell pointer to cell D1. Enter the appropriate formula: +A1+C1−B1 and press <Return>.
- Move the cell pointer to cell D2. Enter the appropriate formula: +C2−B2/A2 and press <Return>.
- Follow the above procedure while entering formulas in cells D3 to D10. Then check to determine if you entered the following formulas correctly.

D3:	+A3*B3
D4:	+C4/A4
D5:	(A5+C5)/B5
D6:	+A6∧2
D7:	(B7+C7)−(A7+B7)
D8:	@SQRT(C8)
D9:	+B9*23
D10:	@SQRT(C10)+@SQRT(B10)

EXERCISE 7 - Using Functional Formulas

- Move the cell pointer to cell G5. Enter the appropriate functional formula to compute the total for row 5. Type @SUM(B5.F5) and press <Return>.
- Move the cell pointer to cell H5. Enter the appropriate functional formula to compute the average for row 5. Type @AVG(B5.F5) and press <Return>.
- Move the cell pointer to cell B12. Enter the appropriate formula. Type @SUM(B5.B10) and press <Return>.
- Move the cell pointer to cell B13. Enter the appropriate functional formula to compute the average for values in column B. Type @AVG(B5.B10) and press <Return>.
- Move the cell pointer to cell B14. Enter the appropriate functional formula to determine the highest value in column B. Type @MAX(B5.B10) and press <Return>.
- Move the cell pointer to cell B15. Enter the appropriate functional formula to determine the lowest value in column B. Type @MIN(B5.B10) and press <Return>.

EXERCISE 8 - Copying Formulas

- Change to Global Fixed Format with 2 decimal places as follows: / Worksheet Global Format Fixed 2 <Return>.
- Move the cell pointer to cell G5. Type / Copy G5.G5 <Return> G6.G10 <Return>. Note: The formula should now be copied from cell G5 into cells G6 to G10.
- Move the cell pointer to cell H5. Repeat the above steps to copy the formula from cell H5 to cells H6 to H10.
- Move the cell pointer to cell B12. Type / Copy B12.B15 <Return> C12.H15 <Return>.
- Remember that you always have the alternative of using the "pointing" or "typing" methods to identify cell ranges. Using the "pointing" method, the above step will be completed as follows: Move the cell pointer to cell B12. Type / C then move the cell

pointer to cell B15 then press <Return> to identify the source range. Move the cell pointer to cell C12, type . (a period), move the cell pointer to cell H15 and then press <Return>. Notice that the answer to the prompt is the same with both methods. Also, notice that the range is highlighted to permit greater accuracy. For this reason, many people prefer the "pointing" method.

EXERCISE 9 - Moving Text and Values and Deleting Columns

- Move the cell pointer to cell A3. Type / Move B3.B14 <Return> A3.A14 <Return> to move the information from column B to column A.
- Move the cell pointer to any cell in column B. Type / Worksheet Delete Column <Return> to delete column B.
- Repeat the above procedure to delete column C.
- Move the cell pointer to cell A3. Type / Move A3.A3 <Return> A4.A4 <Return> to move the text from cell A3 to cell A4.

EXERCISE 10 - Inserting and Deleting Rows

- Move the cell pointer to cell A10. Type / Worksheet Delete Row <Return> to delete row 10.
- Move the cell pointer to cell A8. Type / Worksheet Insert Row <Return> to insert a blank row 8.
- See Exercise 7 for a review of functional formulas and Exercise 8 for a review of copying formulas and Exercise 5 for a review of formatting values.

EXERCISE 11 - Inserting Columns

- Move the cell pointer to cell D1. Type / Worksheet Insert Column <Return> to insert a blank column D.
- Note: Enter \= in cell D2 and enter \- in

cell D4 to make the rulings. Repeat for cells D12 and D14. Notice that the backslash (\) followed by a single character will repeat the character across the cell.

EXERCISE 12 - Providing a Label Prefix

- Move the cell pointer to cell A4. Type / Range Label-Prefix Center A4.B4 <Return> to center the headings for columns A and B.
- Follow the above procedure to center the heading and data for column C. (Remember the ruling in cell C5.)
- Move the cell pointer to cell D4. Type / Range Label-Prefix Right D4.G4 <Return> to right-align the headings for columns D to G.

EXERCISE 13 - Erasing Text and Values

- Move the cell pointer to cell E11. Type / Range Erase E11.E11 <Return> to erase the overtime hours in cell E11.
- Move the cell pointer to cell F6. Type / Range Erase F6.F14 <Return> to erase the values in column F.
- Use the previous procedure to erase the text in column G, except for the column heading.
- Type / Move B2.F15 <Return> A2 <Return> to move all information (except Payroll Record) one column to the left.

EXERCISE 14 - Specifying Global Formats

- Type / Worksheet Global Format Fixed 1 <Return> to change to Global Format with 1 decimal place.
- Use the above procedure for the additional requested formats, but remember that Comma Format requires that the comma symbol , be indicated.

EXERCISE 15 - Providing Range Names

- Type / Range Name Create ONE <Return> B5.B9 <Return> to assign the Range Name ONE to cells B5 to B9.
- Use the above procedure for assigning the Range Names TWO, THREE, and FOUR.
- Type / Range Format Fixed 1 <Return> ONE <Return> to format the values in column B (cells B5 to B9). Note that the Range Name was used instead of the range in the command sequence.
- Use the above procedure to format the values, using range names, in columns C to E.

EXERCISE 16 - Using Parenthesis Hierarchy

- Move the cell pointer to cell E3. Type (A3+B3)/(C3+D3) <Return> to enter the correct formula in cell E3.
- Move the cell pointer to cell E4. Type (A4+C4)*3.43 <Return> to enter the correct formula in cell E4.
- Move the cell pointer to cell E5. Type @SQRT(A5+C5) <Return> to enter the correct formula in cell E5.
- Enter the correct formulas for cells E6 to E8. Remember that the symbol ∧ is used for raising values to powers, such as A1∧3 to raise the value in cell A1 to the third power.

EXERCISE 17 - Integrated Reinforcement

- No new commands were used in this exercise.

EXERCISE 18 - Setting Decimal Places and Formats

- No new commands were used in this exercise.

EXERCISE 19 - Creating Memorandums

- Move the cell pointer to cell A1 and then type / Worksheet Col-Width Set 40 <Return> to widen column A to 40 spaces.
- Note: There was no particular reason for choosing 40 spaces as the column width in this example.
- Move the cell pointer to cell A1 and then type / Range Justify A3.A20 <Return> to justify text material in column A.

EXERCISE 20 - Changing Text Alignment and Formats

- Move the cell pointer to cell A4. Type / Range Label-prefix Center A4.A4 <Return> to center the heading in cell A4.
- Move the cell pointer to cell B4. Type / Range Label-prefix Center B4.B12 <Return> to center the heading and text in cells B4 to B12.
- Use the above procedure to right-align headings in cells C3 to F4.

EXERCISE 21 - Changing Column Widths

- Move the cell pointer to cell A1. Assuming that you decide that column A should be 22 spaces wide, type / Worksheet Col-Width Set 22 <Return>.
- Use the above procedure to widen or narrow (as appropriate) columns B to E.
- Note: As an alternative to typing the desired width of the column, you can use the ← or → key to widen or narrow the column— then press <Return> when the desired width is displayed.

EXERCISE 22 - Printing Headers

- Type / Print Printer Range A1.E18 <Return> Options Header Confidential <Return> Quit Align Go Page Quit to print the report with a heading. Notice that the heading Confidential should have printed at the top of the report.

- Note: To clear all settings (such as print range, headers, footers, and borders), type / Print Printer Clear All Quit.

EXERCISE 23 - Printing Footers

- Type / Print Printer Range A1.E18 <Return> Options Footer Return to Room 2186 <Return> Header Page # <Return> Quit Align Go Page Quit to print the page number as a header at the top of the page and the desired footer at the bottom of the page. Notice that the footer does not print until you use the command to advance the page.

EXERCISE 24 - Printing Borders

- Type / Print Printer Range B1.F18 <Return> Options Borders Columns A1.A16 <Return> Quit Align Go Page Quit to print the Overdue Accounts notation on the border of each page of the report.
- Note: The border (entered in cells A1 to A16) will print on subsequent pages. Likewise, the header and footer will print on subsequent pages of a multipage report. The border can be entered in columns (as illustrated above) or in rows if you want the same border to print on each page. Caution: The border should not be included in the print range or the information will print two times.

EXERCISE 25 - Printing Cell Formulas

- Note: Be sure that the following formula is entered in cell E5: $+B5*C5*D5/365$.
- Type / Print Printer Range A1.F17 <Return> Options Other Cell-Formulas Quit Align Go Page Quit to print the worksheet with cell formulas.
- Note: To return to printing the spreadsheet in the normal manner, type / Print Printer Range A1.F17 <Return> Options Other As-Displayed Quit Align Go Page Quit.

EXERCISE 26 - Changing Margins and Using Data Fill

- Move the cell pointer to cell A6. Type / Data Fill A6.A13 <Return> 1 <Return> 1 <Return> 8 <Return> to have the software automatically number the properties.
- Note: Be sure that the following formula was entered in cell F6: + E6 − D6 − C6.
- Type / Print Printer Range A1.B14 <Return> Options Margins Left 20 <Return> Quit Align Go Page Quit to print the report with a 20-space left margin.

EXERCISE 27 - Protecting Cell Contents

- Enter formulas to compute the average for data in columns C and D, with the average data formatted appropriately.
- Note: The default for global worksheet protection is "Disable," which means that no cells are protected.
- Change the global protection default by entering the following menu command: / Worksheet Global Protection Enable. Note: The entire worksheet is now protected. Try to make a few entries. You should hear a "beep" each time you try to make an entry. Press <Esc> to continue.
- To unprotect all cells except the ones where the averages are located, enter the following command: / Range Unprotect A1.D13 <Return>. Note: The cells in the range A1 to D13 are now unprotected—cells on row 14 remain protected.

EXERCISE 28 - Integrated Reinforcement

- All commands and instructions for completing this exercise have been given previously.

EXERCISE 29 - Using @DATE

- Move the cell pointer to cell C3. Then enter @DATE(89,4,12) to display the date for April 12, 1989 (32610 will appear in the cell).

- Note that the format for @DATE is as follows: @DATE (year-number,month-number,day-number) This translates as @DATE(89,4,12) for April 12, 1989.
- Move the cell pointer to cell A8. Enter the @DATE functional formula to display the date for April 3, 1989. Note: Did you enter @DATE(89,4,3) in cell A8? Continue to enter the @DATE functional formulas for the remaining entries in column A. Then format the range as indicated in the example below.
- Format the date index in cell C3 as follows: / Range Format Date 1 C3.C3< Return>. Then format cells A8 to A15 in a similar manner by typing / Range Format Date 1 A8.A15 <Return>.
- To compute the Percent Change in cell D8, enter (C8 − B8)/B8. Copy the formula as needed. Then format the values for the Percent Format with 1 decimal place.

EXERCISE 30 - Using Date Arithmetic

- Use the @DATE functional formula to enter the dates in cells C6 to C14. Format: @DATE(year-number,month-number,day-number). For example, you would enter @DATE(87,11,23) in cell C6 for November 23, 1987. Continue to enter the dates in the remaining cells in column C. Note: Review Exercise 29, if needed, for the steps to enter and format dates.
- Move the cell pointer to cell E6. Enter a formula to add the contents of cell C6 to the contents of cell D6. Then copy the formula to the remaining cells in column E. Then format the cells in column E to display the dates when the various bonds will mature or become due for payment.

EXERCISE 31 - Finding the Remainder

- Move the cell pointer to cell D6. Enter @MOD(B6,C6) to determine the number of items that will remain if an equal number of the 2,465 items are shipped to each of the 189 stores.

- Note that the format for @MOD is as follows: @MOD(value1,value2).
- Copy the formula in cell D6 to the remaining cells in column D.

EXERCISE 32 - Converting to Integer Values

- Move the cell pointer to cell A10. Enter the formula to convert cell A5 to an integer value: @INT(A5).
- Note that the format for @INT is as follows: @INT(value).
- Then copy the formula to the remaining cells in the range A10 to D13.

EXERCISE 33 - Finding the Highest and Lowest Value

- Move the cell pointer to cell B12. Enter the following formula: @MAX(B5.B10) and press <Return>. The largest value in the range should be displayed in cell B12.
- Note that the formats for @MAX and @MIN are: @MAX(value-range) and @MIN(value-range).
- Move the cell pointer to cell B14. Enter the following formula: @MIN(B5.B10) and press <Return>. The smallest value in the range should be displayed in the cell.

EXERCISE 34 - Counting Values

- Move the cell pointer to cell B16. Enter the following formula: @COUNT(B5.B10) and press <Return>. The number of values in the range should be displayed in the cell.
- Note that the format for @COUNT is: @COUNT(value-range).

EXERCISE 35 - Computing Totals

- This exercise should provide a review for you.
- Move the cell pointer to cell B12. Enter the following formula: @SUM(B5.B10) and

press <Return>. The total of the values in the range should be displayed in the cell.
- Note that the format for @SUM is: @SUM(value-range).

EXERCISE 36 - Computing Averages

- This exercise should provide a review for you.
- Move the cell pointer to cell B15. Enter the following formula: @AVG(B5.B13) and press <Return>. The average of the values in the range should be displayed in the cell.
- Note that the format for @AVG is: @AVG(value-range).
- Review Exercise 33, if needed, to determine the functional formulas needed for cells B17 and B19.

EXERCISE 37 - Computing Periodic Payments

- Move the cell pointer to cell E6. Enter the following formula: @PMT(B6,C6/12,D6) and press <Return>. The monthly payment amount should be displayed in the cell. Note that the cell containing the interest rate was divided by 12 because the rate is based on an annual percentage and payments are made 12 times per year (monthly).
- Note that the format for @PMT is: @PMT(loan-amount,interest-rate,loan-length).
- Copy the formula in cell E6 into cells E7 to E14.
- Review Exercise 35, if needed, to determine the functional formula needed in cell E16 to compute the total.

EXERCISE 38 - Computing Net Present Value

- Move the cell pointer to cell B13. Enter the following formula: @NPV(B11,B5.B9) and press <Return>. The net present value of the five cash flow amounts should be displayed in the cell.

- Note that the format for @NPV is: @NPV(interest-rate,cash-flow-range).
- Copy the formula from cell B13 to cell C13.

EXERCISE 39 - Computing Internal Rate of Return

- Move the cell pointer to cell B12. Enter the following formula: @IRR(0.085,B5.B10) and press <Return>. The internal rate of return should be displayed in the cell.
- Note that the format for @IRR is: @IRR(interest-rate-guess,cash-flow-range).
- Copy the formula in cell B12 into cells C12 to D12.

EXERCISE 40 - Computing Future Value of an Annuity

- Move the cell pointer to cell D6. Enter the following formula: @FV(A6,B6/12,C6*12) and press <Return>. The future value should be displayed in the cell.
- Note that the format for @FV is: @FV (payment-amount,interest-rate,number-of-payments).
- Note that the interest rate was divided by 12 and the number of years was multiplied by 12 to adjust for changing yearly to monthly.
- Copy the formula in cell D6 into cells D7 to D11.
- Note: Widen column D, as needed, to display the values.

EXERCISE 41 - Computing Present Value of an Annuity

- Move the cell pointer to cell D6. Enter the following formula: @PV(A6,C6/12,B6*12) and press <Return>. The amount of money (present value) needed to invest to obtain the indicated payments should be displayed in cell D6.
- Note that the format for @PV is: @PV

(payment-amount,interest-rate,number-of-payments).
- Copy the formula from cell D6 into cells D7 to D11.

EXERCISE 42 - Computing Variance and Standard Deviation

- Enter the formulas for computing the average and high scores in cells F5 and G5. Copy the formulas to the remaining cells through row 17.
- Move the cell pointer to cell B19. Enter the following formula: @VAR(B5.B17) and press <Return>. The variance should be displayed in the cell.
- Note that the format for @VAR is: @VAR(value-range)
- Move the cell pointer to cell B20. Enter the following formula: @STD(B5.B17) and press <Return>. The standard deviation should be displayed in the cell.
- Note that the format for @STD is: @STD(value-range)
- Copy the formulas to the remaining cells in rows 19 and 20.

EXERCISE 43 - Rounding Values

- Move the cell pointer to cell A1. Enter the following functional formula to round the first value: @ROUND(104.5636,3) and press <Return>. Notice that the value displayed in cell A1 is rounded to the indicated number of decimal places (3).
- Note that the format for @ROUND is: @ROUND(value,digits-to-round).
- Repeat the formula, individually, while entering and rounding each of the other values in the exercise in cells A2 to A6.
- Note: In cell A6 enter the following formula in order to round to hundreds: @ROUND(428.892, − 2) and press <Return>. Note that the minus sign (−) causes the value to round to the desired number of places to the left of the decimal place.

EXERCISE 44 - Computing Square Roots

- Move the cell pointer to cell B1. Enter the functional formula that follows to compute the square root: @SQRT(A1) and press <Return>. Note that the square root is displayed in the cell.
- Note that the format for @SQRT is: @SQRT(value).
- Copy the formula from cell B1 into cells B2 to B8.

EXERCISE 45 - Determining Random Numbers

- Move the cell pointer to cell A1. Enter the following functional formula: @RAND and press <Return>. A random number between 0 and 1 should now be displayed in cell A1.
- Copy the formula from cell A1 into cells A2 to A20.
- Move the cell pointer to cell B1. Enter the following functional formula: @RAND*100 and press <Return>. Copy the formula as directed. Format the range as directed.

EXERCISE 46 - Integrated Reinforcement

- No new commands are introduced in exercise. Note that you are requested to save this exercise as EXER47. It will be retrieved for use with Exercise 47.

EXERCISE 47 - Updating Files

- If your instructor has already given directions for file replacement, you may have learned commands for this exercise.
- To save the file with replacement, enter the following command: / File Save EXER47 <Return> Replace.

EXERCISE 48 - File List and File Erase

- To list the worksheet files on the screen, enter the following command: / File List Worksheet.
- Press <Esc> to return to the worksheet.
- To delete the file EXER47 from the disk, enter the following command: / File Erase Worksheet EXER47 <Return> Yes.
- Note that the worksheet still remains on the screen and in memory even though it has been erased from disk storage.

EXERCISE 49 - Combining Worksheets

- Create and save the two worksheets as directed.
- Retrieve file A49 as directed.
- Move the cell pointer to cell A10. To combine file B49 with A49, enter the following command: / File Combine Copy Entire B49 and press <Return>. Notice that the entries from file B49 should appear beginning in cell A10. The two files are now combined.

EXERCISE 50 - Freezing Titles

- Move the cell pointer to cell A6. To freeze the titles (rows 1 to 5), enter the following command: / Worksheet Titles Horizontal.
- Note that you will not notice a change in the worksheet appearance at this time. However, the titles will "freeze" on the screen for easier entry beyond row 20.
- Enter and copy the formula needed to compute the overall average for the 30 students.
- Note: If you desire to clear the titles after the exercise is completed, enter the following command: / Worksheet Titles Clear.

EXERCISE 51 - Using Multiple Windows

- Review Exercise 50, if needed, for commands necessary for freezing titles.
- Move the values as directed. As you move

beyond row 20, notice that the top rows scroll upward and out of view.

- To divide the screen into two windows, move the cell pointer to cell A11 and enter the following command: / Worksheet Windows Horizontal.
- Note: Press <F6> to move from one window to another.
- Note: If you desire to restore the screen to one window, enter the following command: / Worksheet Windows Clear.

EXERCISE 52 - Printing Page Numbers

- Note: This activity was presented in Exercise 22. If needed, review Exercise 22 to print page numbers as headers.

EXERCISE 53 - Using Vertical Table Lookup

- Move the cell pointer to cell A14, where the first value from the table is to be displayed.
- To look up the cost price for product 64327, enter the following command: @VLOOKUP(64327,A6.C12,1). The cost price of the product should be displayed in cell A14.
- Notice that the @VLOOKUP functional formula format is entered as follows: @VLOOKUP(selector-value,lookup-range,offset-column).
- Enter the remaining functional formulas as directed in the exercise. As a checkup, did you enter @VLOOKUP(83528,A6.C12,2) to perform the directed lookup in cell A17?

EXERCISE 54 - Using Horizontal Table Lookup

- Move the cell pointer to cell A8, where the first value from the table is to be displayed.
- To look up the current wage for employee 303, enter the following command: @HLOOKUP(303,B3.G5,1). The current wage

of the employee should be displayed in cell A8.

- Notice that the @HLOOKUP functional formula format is entered as follows: @HLOOKUP(selector-value,lookup-range,offset-row).
- Enter the remaining functional formulas as directed in the exercise. As a checkup, did you enter @HLOOKUP(301,B3.G5,2) to perform the lookup directed in cell B9?

EXERCISE 55 - Using Manual Calculation

- The default for calculation is "automatic." To verify your default settings, enter / Worksheet Status.
- After returning to your screen, enter the following command to switch calculation to "manual": / Worksheet Global Recalculation Manual.
- Notice that calculations are not automatically completed as you copy formulas. After all formulas have been entered and/or copied, press <F9> to manually initiate calculation.
- Note: If you are in the manual calculation mode, <F9> can be pressed at any time to initiate calculation. To get back to the automatic calculation mode, enter / Worksheet Global Recalculation Automatic.

EXERCISE 56 - Making an ASCII File

- Note: A file should be saved in the ASCII format if the file will be retrieved into another document format, such as a word-processing document.
- To save the file in the ASCII format, enter the following command: / Print File EXER56 <Return> Range A1.D15 <Return> Align Go Quit.
- Note: The file should now be saved on the disk in an ASCII format. Enter / File List Print to view the ASCII file(s) on the screen. Notice that this type of file has PRN for an extension. Press <Esc> to return to the worksheet.

EXERCISE 57 - Integrated Reinforcement

- No new commands are introduced in this exercise.

EXERCISE 58 - Using Single Variable Values

- Move the cell pointer to cell E6. The following logical formula should be entered: @IF(D6=5,1,0).
- Notice that the @IF functional formula format is entered as follows: @IF(argument, true-condition,false-condition). In other words, if the value in cell D6 equals 5, a 1 will be placed in the cell (a true condition). Otherwise, a 0 will be placed in the cell (a false condition). The @IF functional formula is used to make decisions.
- Practice by entering the @IF functional formula in cell E7 to make sure that you understand the formula. Then copy the formula to the remaining cells in column E.
- Move the cell pointer to cell F6. The following logical formula should be entered: @IF(D6>5,1,0).

EXERCISE 59 - Using Logical Operators

- Move the cell pointer to cell E6. The following logical formula should be entered: @IF(D6<=5,C6+5,C6+10).
- Practice by entering the formula in cell E7. Then copy the formula to the remaining cells in column E.

EXERCISE 60 - Using Logical Operators with Math

- Move the cell pointer to cell D6. The following logical formula should be entered: @IF(B6>30,C6*0.25,C6*0.10).
- Practice by entering the formula in cell D7. Then copy the formula to the remaining cells in column D.
- Complete the worksheet by entering and

copying formulas in columns E and F and in row 16.

EXERCISE 61 - Using a Logical Connective: OR

- Move the cell pointer to cell E6. The following logical formula should be entered: @IF(B6>29#OR#C6>54,1,0).
- Practice by entering the formula in cell E7. Then copy the formula to the remaining cells in column E (through row 12).
- Enter the @SUM functional formula in cell E14 to compute the number eligible for retirement.

EXERCISE 62 - Using a Logical Connective: AND

- Move the cell pointer to cell D6. The following locical formula should be entered: @IF(B6>10#AND#C6>1000,A6,0).
- Practice by entering the formula in cell D7. Then copy the formula to the remaining cells in column D.

EXERCISE 63 - Integrated Reinforcement

- No new commands are introduced in this exercise.

EXERCISE 64 - Using a Range Format Macro

- Move the cell pointer to cell A11. Enter the following macro in cell A11: ' / Range Format Currency 2 ~ A3.A8 ~/. Note: This is called "creating" the macro. Notice that the keystrokes are entered in the macro as they would have been entered if the application was actually being performed. The tilde (~) must be used in place of a <Return> in a macro.
- Move the cell pointer to cell C11. Enter A in the cell. Note: This is an optional step that indicates the name that will later be used for the macro.

- Move the cell pointer to cell D11. Enter <u>Macro to format column A, Currency, 2 decimals.</u> This is also an optional step that describes what the macro will do when executed.
- Move the cell pointer to cell A11 where the macro is located. Enter the following command: <u>/ Range Name Create \A <Return> A11.A11</u> <Return>. Note: This is called "naming" the macro.
- Press <Alt> and <u>A</u>. Column A should be formatted immediately after you perform this step. Note: This is called "invoking" the macro.
- Review: For each macro, you should create it, name it, and invoke it. For documentation purposes, you should also indicate the name in a nearby cell and a short description in a nearby cell.
- Follow the above procedure for creating, naming, and invoking the remaining macros requested in the exercise.
- Note: The backslash (\) must be used in front of each macro when naming the macro. The name of the macro should be a single letter of the alphabet, with a few exceptions. If you save this worksheet, use a name other than EXER64, since this template will be used for several exercises that follow.

EXERCISE 65 - Using an Erase Worksheet Macro

- Review the steps for creating, naming, and invoking a macro which were illustrated in Exercise 64.
- Note: Did you create your macro as follows: <u>'/WEY?</u>

EXERCISE 66 - Using a Print Macro

- Review the steps for creating, naming, and invoking a macro which were illustrated in Exercise 64.
- Note: Did you create the macro as follows: <u>'/PPRA1.E9 ~ AGPQ?</u>

EXERCISE 67 - Using a Special Key Macro

- Review the steps for creating, naming, and invoking a macro which were illustrated in Exercise 64.
- Note: Did you create the macro in cell A11 as follows: <u>{HOME}</u>?
- Note: Did you create the macro in cell A13 as follows: <u>{GOTO}E6~54.78~{HOME}</u>?

EXERCISE 68 - Using an Interactive Pause Macro

- This worksheet shows a macro that will permit you to make the desired entry and simply press <Return> to move on to the next entry.
- Move the cell pointer to cell A5 prior to invoking the macro.
- Note: Enter <u>/ Quit No</u> to exit from macro control. Otherwise, you will not be able to stop execution of the macro.
- You are also instructed to add a print macro. Review Exercise 66, if needed, when creating the print macro.

EXERCISE 69 - Using an Interactive Pause Macro

- Enter a macro similar to the one presented in Exercise 68. However, this macro will direct the cell pointer "down" instead of "right," which was needed for Exercise 68.
- Remember that you can stop macro execution by entering <u>/QN</u>.
- Note: You will invoke the macro, enter all the names, then enter the scores, and exit the macro control.

EXERCISE 70 - Using Intelligent Macros

- Did you enter the following macro in cell A15: <u>'/RF,0~{?}~</u>
- Enter the remaining macro. Remember to

place a question mark inside the brackets to indicate a pause.

EXERCISE 71 - Using an Automatic Execution Macro

- Move the cell pointer to cell A19. Enter a normal print macro. Review Exercise 66, if needed, for instructions for writing a print macro.
- After creating the macro, you should name the macro 0 so that it will automatically be executed each time you retrieve the worksheet. Note: This particular name indicates to the software that the macro should be invoked each time the file is retrieved.
- To test the macro, save the file. Be sure that your printer is ready prior to retrieving the file. Then retrieve the file.

EXERCISE 72 - Developing a Master Macro File

- Instructions from previous exercises should provide sufficient instructions needed to create the macros requested for this exercise.
- The master macro file, once developed, can serve as a source for macros needed for other worksheet applications. A macro created in the master macro file can be retrieved into other worksheets as needed, to avoid writing the same macros for each worksheet created.

EXERCISE 73 - Using Master Macros

- Move the cell pointer to cell A19. Enter the following command to extract the macro: / File Combine Copy Named PRINT <Return> MACRO <Return>.
- The print macro from the master file should now be displayed on row 19. Note: The name given to the macro in the master file does not transfer to this file so you will have to name the macro in this file in the usual manner.

EXERCISE 74 - Integrated Reinforcement

- No new commands are introduced in this exercise.

EXERCISE 75 - Constructing a Database

- The worksheet created in this exercise will be used as a database in Exercises 76 to 83.
- Entries in rows 9 to 18 are the records in the database.
- Each column heading identifies a field or item of information in a record. There are 7 fields represented on row 6.
- With these fields used as a reference, records can be sorted, found, extracted, or deleted from the database.

EXERCISE 76 - Sorting Numerically

- To sort the database numerically by student number, type / Data Sort Data-range A9.G18 <Return> Primary-key A6 <Return> Ascending <Return>.
- Type Go and the records should appear in numeric sequence by student number.
- To sort the database numerically by section within each grade, type / Data Sort Data-range A9.G18 <Return>.
- Type Primary-key E6 <Return> Ascending <Return> Secondary-key F6 <Return> Ascending <Return> Go.
- The records should now appear in numeric sequence by section within each grade.

EXERCISE 77 - Sorting Alphabetically

- To sort the records alphabetically by last names and first names within each last name, type / Data Sort Data-range A9.G18 <Return> Primary-key B6 <Return> Ascending <Return> Secondary-key C6 <Return> Ascending <Return> Go.

EXERCISE 78 - Finding Records

- When finding all records for students with the last name Loflin, first create a criterion range by typing / Copy A6.G6 <Return> A25.G25 <Return>.
- Press <PgDn> to view the criterion range in cells A25 to G25.
- Move the cell pointer to cell B26 and type Loflin <Return> as the criteria to search for in the database.
- Press <Home>.
- To find selected records, type / Data Query Input A6.G18 <Return> Criterion B25.B26 <Return> Find.
- The first record for Loflin should appear highlighted on the screen.
- Press the ↓ key to find the next record for Loflin.
- Continue to press the ↓ key until a "beep" sounds indicating that there are no more records in the database matching the criteria specified.
- Press <Esc> to finish the data query. Type Quit to leave the menu.
- To find records for all students in Grade 11, move the cell pointer to cell B26 and type / Range Erase <Return>. This should clear the criterion range from the previous data query.
- Move the cell pointer to cell E26 and type 11 <Return> to establish the criteria to be used in the search for Grade 11 students.
- Press <Home>.
- To find the records matching the selected criteria, type / Data Query Input A6.G18 <Return> Criterion E25.E26 <Return> Find.
- The first record for a Grade 11 student should appear highlighted on the screen.
- Press the ↓ key to view other records matching the criteria specified. When the "beep" sounds, press <Esc> to finish the data query.
- Type Quit to leave the menu.

EXERCISE 79 - Finding Records Using Logical Relationships

- Move the cell pointer to cell A25 to view

and check the criterion range in cells A25 to G25.
- If needed, erase any entries previously made in cells A26 to G26.
- When a search is performed using logical criteria, there can be no entries or blank rows between the column headings and the first record in the database.
- Move the cell pointer to cell A7 and type / Worksheet Delete Row <Down> <Return>. This should delete rows 7 and 8 from the spreadsheet.
- Move the cell pointer to cell A25 and notice that the criterion range now starts in A23 instead of A25.
- Move the cell pointer to cell G24 and type +G7>3.5 <Return> to establish the criteria to search for.
- Notice that the contents of cell G24 will appear as 1 at this time. With the cell pointer on cell G24 type / Range Format Text <Return> to display the logical criteria in cell G24.
- Press <Home>.
- Type / Data Query Input A6.G16 <Return> Criterion G23.G24 <Return> Find.
- Press <Down> to view each record matching the specified criteria.
- When the "beep" sounds, press <Esc> to finish the data query. Type Quit to leave the menu.
- To change the logical criteria, move the cell pointer to cell G24 and type +G7<3 <Return>. Press <Home>.
- Since the only change in this and the previous data query is the logical criteria, the Query key can be used to find the selected records matching the criteria.
- Press <F7> (the Query key) to complete the data query.
- View the records as they are highlighted on the screen, and press <Esc> to finish the data query.

EXERCISE 80 - Extracting Records

- Move the cell pointer to cell A25 to view and check the criterion range.
- If needed, erase any entries in cells A26 to G26 to clear the criterion range.

- If the criterion range does not exist, create the criterion range by copying cells A6 to G6 into cells A25 to G25.
- To create the extraction output range, copy the contents of cells A6 to G6 into cells A30 to G30.
- Move the cell pointer to cell E26 and type 10 <Return> to establish the criteria for the extraction. Press <Home>.
- To extract all records for students in Grade 10, type / Data Query Input A6.G18 <Return> Criterion E25.E26 <Return> Output A30.G40 <Return> Extract Quit.
- Press <PgDn> to view the extracted output range. Only records for students in Grade 10 should appear.
- To print the extracted records, print the range A30 to G40 to include the heading information.
- To change the extraction criteria, move the cell pointer to cell E26 and type 11 <Return>.
- Press <F7> to repeat the extraction command for Grade 11 students.
- Print the extracted output range.
- Change the extraction criteria in cell E26 by typing 12 <Return>.
- Press <F7> to repeat the extraction command for Grade 12 students.

EXERCISE 81 - Using Multiple Criteria

- If needed, clear any entries previously made in the criterion range A26 to G26.
- To establish the multiple criteria, move the cell pointer to cell E26 and type 12 <Return>.
- Move the cell pointer to cell F26 and type 8 <Return>.
- In order for a record to be extracted, both criteria must be met.
- Type the command for extracting records using E25.F26 <Return> to expand the criterion range to include both criteria.
- Complete the extraction and printing.
- Move the cell pointer to cell F26 and erase the cell contents.
- Move the cell pointer to cell G26 and type 4.00 <Return>.   Cell E26 should still

contain 12. This establishes the multiple criterion of 12 and 4.00.
- Type the command for extracting records using E25.G26 <Return> to expand the criterion range to include both criteria.
- Complete the extraction and printing.

EXERCISE 82 - Eliminating Duplicate Records

- Create the criterion range and extraction output range by copying cells A6 to D6 into cells A17 to D17 and also into A20 to D20.
- Move the cell pointer to cell C18, type +C7<30 and press <Return>.
- Format the entry in cell C18 for Text Format.
- To extract only unique records matching the criteria specified, type / Data Query Input A6.D14 <Return> Criterion C17.C18 <Return> Output A20.D30 <Return> Unique Quit.
- Move the cell pointer to cell A23 to view and examine the extracted records. There should be no duplicate records.
- To delete the unwanted record from the database, delete the row containing the record.

EXERCISE 83 - Deleting Records

- Deleting selected records from a database is a maintenance feature to keep up-to-date records.
- Check and clear the criterion range of any previous entries.
- In cell E26 type 10 <Return> to establish the criteria for deleting records.
- To delete the selected records, type / Data Query Input A6.G18 <Return> Criterion E25.E26 <Return> Delete Delete Quit.
- Press <PgDn> and notice that the deleting of records from the database does not affect the entries in the criterion and output ranges.
- If needed, delete rows 7 and 8 from the worksheet prior to using the logical criteria for deleting records for students with a GPA less than 3.00.

- In cell G24 type $+G7<3$ <Return> to establish the criteria for deleting records.
- Format cell G24 for Text Format. Press <Home>.
- To delete the selected records, type / Data Query Input A6.G14 <Return> Criterion G23.G24 <Return> Delete Delete Quit.
- Notice that the input range automatically adjusted from A6.G18 to A6.G14 after the records for Grade 10 were deleted.

EXERCISE 84 - Statistical Function @DSUM

- The formulas in column H should be entered prior to entering the @DSUM statistical function in cell D17.
- Create the criterion range by copying cells A5 to H5 into cells A20 to H20.
- In cell C21 type LA <Return> to establish the criteria.
- To calculate the total yearly sales for *only* the state of Louisiana, move the cell pointer to cell D17.
- Type the following statistical function: @DSUM($A$5.$H$15,7,$C$20.$C$21) <Return>.
- The first range in the function represents the Input Range, 7 is the offset or column containing the values to be added, and the last range is the criterion range.
- Note: The offset is 7 because column A is considered zero (0).
- Move the cell pointer to cell C17 and type LA <Return> prior to printing the worksheet.
- To calculate the total yearly sales for *only* the state of Texas, change the criteria in cell C21 to TX <Return>.
- Move the cell pointer to cell C17 and type TX <Return> prior to printing the worksheet.

EXERCISE 85 - Statistical Function @DAVG

- If needed, create the criterion range by copying cells A5 to H5 into cells A20 to H20.

- Move the cell pointer to cell A17 and type AVERAGE FOR STATE OF <Return>.
- Move the cell pointer to cell C17 and type FL <Return>.
- In cell C21 type FL <Return> to establish the criteria.
- In cell D17 enter the following @DAVG($A$5.$H$15,7,$C$20.$C$21) <Return> to calculate the average yearly sales for the state of Florida.
- Change the criteria in cell C21 to GA <Return> to calculate the average yearly sales for the state of Georgia.
- In cell C17 type GA <Return>.

EXERCISE 86 - Integrated Reinforcement

- All functions required to complete this exercise have been introduced previously.

EXERCISE 87 - Entering Data for the Graph

- The information in this worksheet will be used to create graphs in Exercises 88 to 92.
- All functions required to complete this exercise have been introduced previously.

EXERCISE 88 - Constructing a Pie Chart

- To create the pie chart, type / Graph Type Pie X B4.C4 <Return> A B13.C13 <Return> Options Titles First CRESTMONT ELEMENTARY SCHOOL <Return> Titles Second Fall Enrollment Summary <Return> Quit Save PIE88 <Return> Quit.
- If you are using a graphics monitor, you may select View to see the pie chart on the screen at any time as it is being created.
- To create the second pie chart, enter the / Graph command above using A6.A11 <Return> for the X data range and D6.D11 <Return> for the A data range. Save the second pie chart as PIE88B.
- Both pie charts, PIE88 and PIE88B, can be printed at the same time since it is necessary to exit 1-2-3 to print graphs.

- Note: If you are using VP-Planner, ready the printer and type Print instead of typing Save PIE88 for the first pie chart above. You do not save the graph or exit the worksheet to print the graph. If using VP-Planner, omit all instructions given below except the next instruction.
- Save the worksheet as EXER88.
- To print the pie chart, exit the 1-2-3 display by typing / Quit Yes.
- When the Access menu appears, remove the Lotus system disk and insert the PrintGraph disk in Drive A.
- Type PrintGraph, and the PrintGraph menu should appear.
- Note: It is assumed that the *configuration* has been completed and saved on the PrintGraph disk to specify the drive for pictures, the drive for fonts, and the printer to be used.
- Type Select to specify the graph to be printed. Use the arrow key to move the cursor next to the graph called PIE88, and press the <Space Bar>. A # sign should appear next to the graph name.
- Press <Return> to select this graph to be printed.
- In the same manner, place a # sign next to the graph name PIE88B to select it for printing.
- Ready the printer and type Go to begin printing the graphs.
- After printing is completed, type Quit to exit the PrintGraph menu and return to the Lotus Access Menu.

EXERCISE 89 - Constructing a Bar Graph

- To construct the bar graph, type / Graph Type Bar X A6.A11 <Return> A D6.D11 <Return> Options Titles First CRESTMONT ELEMENTARY SCHOOL <Return> Titles Second Fall Enrollment Summary <Return> Quit Save BAR89 <Return>. Note: Select View from the menu prior to Quit below to see the completed graph, if you are using a graphics monitor.
- Note: Remember that you do not save

graphs or exit to PrintGraph if you are using VP-Planner. Instead, select P to print the graph. If you are using a graphics monitor, an alternative for printing the graph is to view the graph on the monitor and press <Shift> + <PrtSc> to print the graph from the screen.
- If you are printing using PrintGraph, it will save time to create the second bar graph prior to printing.
- Type the / Graph command changing the X data range to A6.A11 <Return> and changing the A data range to C6.C11 <Return>. Change the second title to Female Fall Enrollment and press <Return>. Save the second bar graph as BAR89B <Return>.
- Type Quit to leave the Graph menu, and save the worksheet as EXER89.
- Print the two bar graphs using the PrintGraph disk. (See Exercise 88 for detailed instructions for printing graphs.)

EXERCISE 90 - Constructing a Multiple Bar Graph

- To create the multiple bar graph, type / Graph Type Bar X A6.A11 <Return> A B6.B11 <Return> B C6.C11 <Return> Options Data-labels A B4.B4 <Return> Above Data-labels B C4.C4 <Return> Above Titles First CRESTMONT ELEMENTARY SCHOOL <Return> Titles Second Male and Female Enrollment <Return> Quit Save BAR90 <Return>.
- Note: Select View from the menu prior to Quit below to see the completed graph if you are using a graphics monitor.
- Note: Review the instructions for printing the graph if you are using VP-Planner. Remember that you do not include commands to save the graph or use PrintGraph commands if you are using VP-Planner. Omit all of the following instructions, except for the next three.
- Type Quit to leave the Graph menu.
- Save the worksheet as EXER90.
- Print the multiple bar graph using the PrintGraph disk. (See Exercise 88 for detailed instructions for printing graphs.)

EXERCISE 91 - Using Legends

- The multiple bar graph shows two bar patterns. The legends should serve to distinguish these two patterns without requiring data labels above the bars.
- The graph settings used to create BAR90 may still exist when the / Graph command is issued. However, reenter the / Graph command with the additions shown below to clear previous data labels and add the legends.
- Type / Graph Reset Graph Type Bar A B6.B11 <Return> B C6.C11 <Return> Options Titles First CRESTMONT ELEMENTARY SCHOOL <Return> Titles Second Male and Female Enrollment <Return> Legend A Males <Return> B Females <Return> Quit Save BAR91 <Return>.
- Type View if you are using a graphics monitor and wish to view the graph on your display screen.
- Note: Review the instructions for printing the graph if you are using VP-Planner. (See Exercise 88 for specific instructions.)
- Type Quit to leave the Graph menu.
- Save the spreadsheet as EXER91.
- Print the graph with legends using the PrintGraph disk.

EXERCISE 92 - Using Axis Titles

- The graph settings for the multiple bar graph with legends should still exist when the / Graph command is entered. If not, reenter the / Graph command as shown in Exercise 91 with the additions shown below.
- Type / Graph Type Bar Options Titles X-axis Grades 1-6 <Return> Titles Y-axis (Males and Females) <Return> Quit Save BAR92 <Return>.
- Type View if you are using a graphics monitor and wish to view the graph on the display screen.
- Note: Review the instructions for printing the graph if you are using VP-Planner. (See Exercise 88 for specific instructions.)
- Type Quit to leave the Graph menu.

- Save the worksheet as EXER92.
- Print the graph with axis titles using the PrintGraph disk.

EXERCISE 93 - Changing the Scale

- To create the bar graph, type / Graph Type Bar X A6.A11 <Return> A B6.B11 <Return> Options Titles First DOW JONES INDUSTRIAL AVERAGE <Return> Titles Second Point Declines <Return> Scale Y-axis Upper 95 <Return> Quit Quit Save BAR93 <Return>.
- Type View if you are using a graphics monitor and wish to view the graph on the display screen.
- Note: Review the instructions for printing the graph if you are using VP-Planner. (See Exercise 88 for specific instructions.)
- Type Quit to leave the Graph menu.
- Save the worksheet as EXER93.
- Print the graph using the PrintGraph disk.

EXERCISE 94 - Constructing a Multiple Line Graph

- To create the line graph, type / Graph Type Line X A7.A15 <Return> A D7.D15 <Return> B E7.E15 <Return> Options Titles First KENTWELL SOUP COMPANY <Return> Titles Second Quarterly Sales Summary <Return> Titles X-axis Salesperson Numbers <Return> Titles Y-axis (Quarters 1 and 2) <Return> Quit Save LINE94 <Return>.
- If using VP-Planner, see Exercise 89 for printing instructions.
- To create LINE94B, type the / Graph command changing the A data range to F7.F15 <Return> and changing the B data range to G7.G15 <Return>.
- Change the y-axis title to (Quarters 3 and 4) <Return>.
- Save the second line graph as LINE94B <Return>.
- To create LINE94C, type the / Graph command changing the A data range to D7.D15

<Return>, the B data range to E7.E15 <Return>. Type for the C data-range F7.F15 <Return> and type for the D data range G7.G15 <Return>.

- Change the Second title to Yearly Sales Summary <Return>.
- Change the *y*-axis title to (Quarters 1-4) <Return>.
- Save the third line graph as LINE94C <Return>.
- Type Quit to leave the Graph menu.
- Save the worksheet as EXER94.
- Print the three line graphs using the PrintGraph disk.

EXERCISE 95 - Constructing an XY Graph

- To create the XY graph, type / Graph Type XY X B6.B9 <Return> A C6.C9 <Return> Options Data-labels A A6.A9 <Return> Above Quit Titles First HIGHWAY'S USED CAR SALES <Return> Titles Second Weekly Revenue Summary <Return> Titles X-axis Cars Sold <Return> Titles Y-axis (Revenue in Dollars) <Return> Quit Save XY95 <Return>.
- If you are using VP-Planner, see Exercise 89 for printing instructions.
- Type View if you are using a graphics monitor and wish to view the XY graph on the display screen.
- Type Quit to leave the Graph menu.
- Save the worksheet as EXER95.
- Print the XY graph using the PrintGraph disk.

EXERCISE 96 - Integrated Reinforcement

- All functions required to complete this exercise have been introduced previously.

EXERCISE 97 - Payroll Register

- This simplified version of a payroll register provides information needed to maintain payroll records and create weekly payroll checks. A more complete version may contain other items such as name, address, length of service, and deductions.
- Overtime pay will be one and one-half times the pay rate for all hours worked in excess of 40. If the employee did not work in excess of 40 hours during the week, the overtime pay will be 0. Your @IF formula for cell D6 should be written to reflect this pay plan.
- Regular pay will equal the hours worked times the pay rate unless hours have been worked in excess of 40. If hours have been worked in excess of 40, regular pay will equal 40 times the pay rate. Your @IF formula for cell E6 should reflect this plan.
- Gross pay is simply the overtime pay amount plus the regular pay amount.
- Review instructions for Exercises 58 to 63, if needed, for developing @IF formulas.

EXERCISE 98 - Inventory Record

- The inventory record is used to maintain information about individual items of merchandise. This record may also contain information about date of purchase, name of usual supplier, cost and sale price of the item, minimum acceptable inventory level, and other related information.
- The formula in cell D7 should reflect the beginning balance plus units purchased or minus units sold.
- The formula in cell D8 should reflect the prior balance plus units purchased or minus units sold. You can then copy this formula from cell D8 into the remaining cells in the column.

EXERCISE 99 - Mortgage Payment Schedule

- A mortgage payment schedule is an essential document when making installment or mortgage purchases. Typical purchases include buying an automobile, furniture, and a new house.
- The payment amount can be computed by using the @PMT functional formula. Re-

view instructions in Exercise 37, if needed.

- You will need to multiply the length of the loan (years) by 12, since the worksheet deals with *monthly* payments.
- Part of each payment represents interest and part of the payment represents a reduction in the loan balance. Use the simple interest formula to determine the amount that should be applied to interest—+$E$3*$E$5/12—in cell C12. The amount that should be applied to principal then equals the difference between the payment amount and the interest applied. The loan balance equals the previous balance less the amount applied to principal. See Exercise 98 for an example of how to handle beginning balances.
- After completing the formulas for row 13, you can copy the formulas into the remaining cells in columns B to E.

EXERCISE 100 - Accounting Income Statement

- This simplified version of an income statement shows the progress of the business over a period of time. This type of statement may be prepared weekly, monthly, quarterly, and/or annually.
- Gross profit is computed by deducting the cost of goods sold from the sales revenue. Net income is computed by deducting total operating expenses from the gross profit amount.
- Percent of sales is computed by dividing each item amount by the sales amount.

EXERCISE 101 - Personal Budget

- A budget is designed to help people, and businesses, plan expenses for a given period of time, such as a week, month, or year. Actual expenses at the end of the period can then be compared with the planned expenses to determine how closely planned and actual amounts are in agreement.
- The amount of income that remains each month is placed into savings in this example. The formula in cell B19 should compute the sum of the expenditures, including savings. The formula in cell B16 should then deduct total expenses (cell B19) from income available (cell E6).
- Percent of income is computed by dividing individual expenditure amounts by the income available amount. If you use the cell address for income available in the formula, be sure to make the address absolute, such as $E$6

Exercise Log

	Exercise No.	Exercise Title	Page	Date Completed	Evaluation
OVERVIEW OF BASICS	1	Entering Text and Values	00	_____	_____
	2	Using Label Prefixes and Saving a File	00	_____	_____
	3	Retrieving and Printing a Worksheet	00	_____	_____
	4	Using the Help Facility with Lotus 1-2-3	00	_____	_____
	5	Formatting Values	00	_____	_____
	6	Entering Formulas	00	_____	_____
	7	Using Functional Formulas	00	_____	_____
	8	Copying Formulas	00	_____	_____
	9	Moving Text and Values and Deleting Columns	00	_____	_____
	10	Inserting and Deleting Rows	00	_____	_____
	11	Inserting Columns	00	_____	_____
	12	Providing a Label Prefix	00	_____	_____
	13	Erasing Text and Values	00	_____	_____
	14	Specifying Global Formats	00	_____	_____
	15	Providing Range Names	00	_____	_____
	16	Using Parenthesis Hierarchy	00	_____	_____
	17	Integrated Reinforcement	00	_____	_____
APPEARANCE OF REPORTS	18	Setting Decimal Places and Formats	00	_____	_____
	19	Creating Memorandums	00	_____	_____
	20	Changing Text Alignment and Formats	00	_____	_____

Appendix

The following list identifies all of the files contained on the data disk for *101 Advanced Spreadsheet Exercises*.

EXER5.WKS	EXER39.WKS
EXER6.WKS	EXER40.WKS
EXER7.WKS	EXER41.WKS
EXER9.WKS	EXER42.WKS
EXER10.WKS	EXER50.WKS
EXER11.WKS	EXER51.WKS
EXER12.WKS	EXER53.WKS
EXER13.WKS	EXER54.WKS
EXER14.WKS	EXER55.WKS
EXER15.WKS	EXER58.WKS
EXER16.WKS	EXER59.WKS
EXER18.WKS	EXER60.WKS
EXER19.WKS	EXER61.WKS
EXER20.WKS	EXER62.WKS
EXER22.WKS	EXER64.WKS
EXER23.WKS	EXER68.WKS
EXER24.WKS	EXER69.WKS
EXER25.WKS	EXER70.WKS
EXER26.WKS	EXER71.WKS
EXER27.WKS	EXER73.WKS
EXER28.WKS	EXER75.WKS
EXER29.WKS	EXER82.WKS
EXER30.WKS	EXER84.WKS
EXER31.WKS	EXER86.WKS
EXER32.WKS	EXER87.WKS
EXER33.WKS	EXER93.WKS
EXER34.WKS	EXER95.WKS
EXER35.WKS	EXER96.WKS
EXER36.WKS	MACRO.WKS
EXER37.WKS	README.WKS
EXER38.WKS	